ARCANA MUNDI

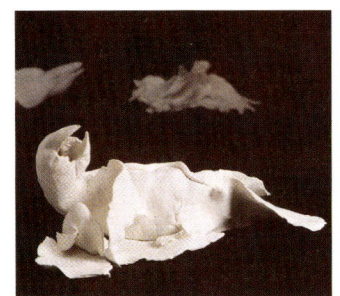

birdfish   *my other tongue*

ARCANA MUNDI

Jan Harrison

SELECTED WORKS

1979–2000

Essay by Linda Weintraub

STATION HILL / BARRYTOWN, LTD.

Published by Station Hill / Barrytown, Ltd.
in Barrytown, NY 12507.

E-mail: publishers@stationhill.org
Online catalogue: http//:www.stationhill.org

Station Hill Arts is a project of The Institute for Publishing Arts, Inc., a not-for-profit, federally tax exempt organization in Barrytown, New York, which gratefully acknowledges ongoing support for its publishing program from the New York State Council on the Arts.

Essay by Linda Weintraub.
New York based independent curator and author

An abbreviated version of the essay, "Genus Fusion," 1998, was originally published in the book ANIMAL.ANIMA.ANIMUS, Pori Art Museum Publications, Pori, Finland, and FRAME Publications, Helsinki, Finland.

The introduction of "Genus Fusion" was published in 1999 in the announcement for the solo exhibition, "Arcana Mundi," at the Alice F. and Harris K. Weston Art Gallery, Aronoff Center for the Arts, Cincinnati, Ohio.

Photographers:
Douglas Baz, *Barrytown, New York (pages 3, 6)*
Nancy Donskoj, *Kingston, New York (pages 13, 16, 17, 18, 19, 25, 27, 40)*
Ron Forth, *Lafayette, Colorado (pages 28, 29, 30, 31, 36, 37, and *Tongue Drawing)*
Erkki Valli-Jaakola, *Pori, Finland (page 22)*
Marlis Momber, *New Paltz, New York (pages 1, 11, 14, 15, 20, 21)*
Tony Walsh, *Cincinnati, Ohio (pages 22, 23, 33, 35)*
*Outdoor water fountain for installation of Tongue Drawing loaned by Murdock Inc., Cincinnati, Ohio.

Designed by Bloodhorse Visions, *New Paltz, New York.*
Text is set in Spectrum and Gill Sans Light, with dreams and journal entries in upside-down hand printing by Jan Harrison.

Printed by State Color, *Schenectady, New York, on Mohawk 50/10 Plus paper.*

The artist's dreams and journal entries are from 1979-1999.
Front and back covers: altered details of INSTINCT DREAM, 1998.
Photograph on outside back cover: JAN HARRISON, ca.1950, West Palm Beach, Florida (photographer unknown).

Library of Congress Cataloging-in-Publication Data

Harrison, Jan, 1944-
    Arcana mundi : selected works, 1979-2000 / Jan Harrison ; text by Linda Weintraub
        p. cm.
    ISBN 1-58177-064-2 (alk. paper)
    1. Harrison, Jan, 1944----Catalogs. I. Weintraub, Linda. II. Title.

    N6537.H3623 A4 2000
    700'.92--dc21

                                                        00-044412

Manufactured in the United States of America

Acknowledgements

Jan Harrison wishes to express gratitude to Alan Baer, for his constant support, assistance, advice and vision, so necessary to the inception and growth of her work, to Linda Weintraub, for her essay, as well as her insight and encouragement, to Ann Pollak, for her longterm support, knowledge, and editorial assistance, to Carolee Schneemann for her advice and mutual kinship and empathy with animals, to Naomi Schechter for her fellowship and good faith, to Catherine Keller and Jason Starr, for past and present support, knowledge, and for Catherine's suggestion of the title for the painting, "Chaosmos." The artist also wishes to thank Susan Quasha and George Quasha at Station Hill/ Barrytown, Ltd. for their valued assistance, and for publishing Arcana Mundi.

I WAS WALKING BY A RIVER, AND I CAME UPON
A BIRD. THE BIRD WAS VERY BEAUTIFUL,
AND VERY PERFECT. I WANTED TO TALK
TO THE BIRD BUT I DIDN'T KNOW HOW.
I LOOKED DOWN AND SAW THAT AROUND THE
BIRD'S NECK WAS A SHINY MEDALLION.
THEN I SAW THAT AROUND MY OWN NECK
WAS A SHINY MEDALLION. I TOUCHED THE
MEDALLIONS TOGETHER, AND AT THAT MOMENT
THE BIRD BEGAN TO SING IN A LANGUAGE
I UNDERSTOOD. I LOOKED DOWN AGAIN AND
SAW THAT THE BIRD'S FEET WERE BECOMING
PAWS OR HANDS.

1979 dream

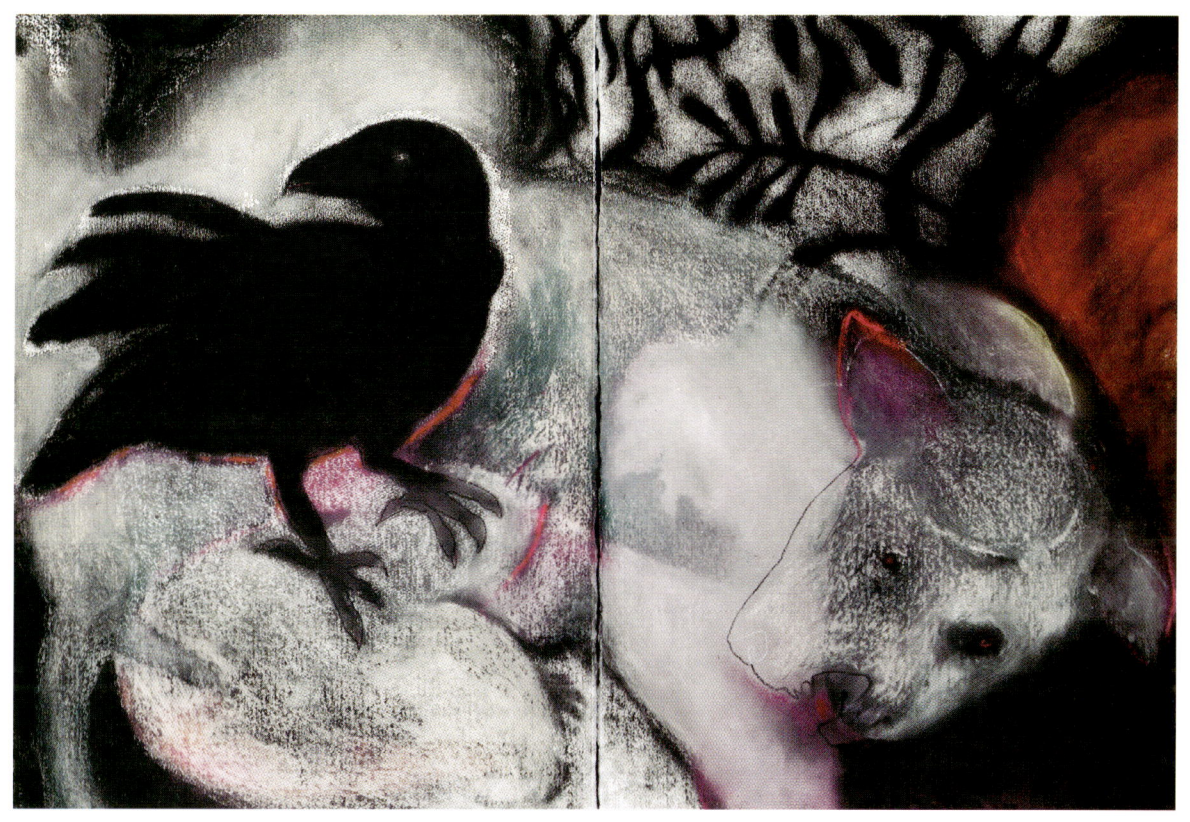

INSTINCT DREAM
1998
charcoal, oilstick and pastel on rag paper
$30^{1}/_{4}$ x $44^{1}/_{2}$ inches
(diptych)

a perilous eden   *this* and *THIS*

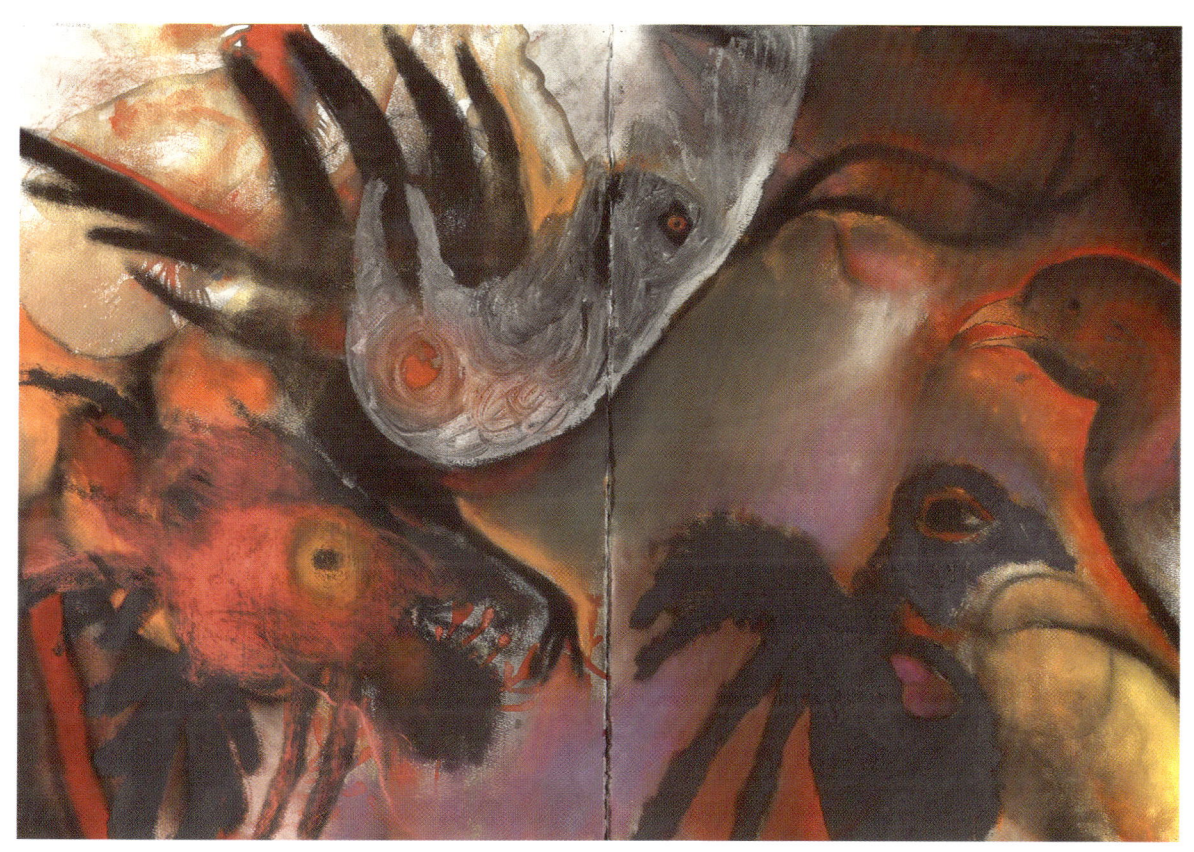

CHAOSMOS
2000
pastel, charcoal and oilstick on rag paper
30^1/4 x 44^1/2 inches
(diptych)

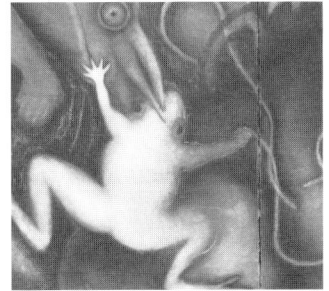

Baubo   *My other tongue is hairy.*

GENUS FUSION
THE ART OF JAN HARRISON

Linda Weintraub

INTRODUCTION

Jan Harrison beckons viewers to embark on a voyage. But instead of leaving home to explore exotic sites and sounds, we are guided into equally foreign territory—our innermost selves. We journey downward, circumventing our personalities and our individual life stories, passing our accumulated recollections and our acquired attitudes, crossing beyond spoken and written histories and even beyond human ancestry. Ultimately we disembark in the wondrous galaxy we carry within each gene. Its constellations are measured in units of shudders, murmurs, gasps, and shivers.

On this primal level, we discover our common animal ancestry, a vestigial remnant here awakened and made observable as pastel drawings, porcelain sculptures, and recorded voices. All three media provide compelling evidence of our membership within the animal kingdom. These visual, tactile, and aural expressions are all discovered during the artist's own inward journey. Through the working process, Harrison probes and ultimately strips away the accreted layers of recorded time. She sheds these confining envelopes, exposing body and psyche to uncompromising nakedness. But once she has arrived at her destination, the material seems to spring into being with the force of an inevitable and authentic stimulus.

This untamed domain is neither malevolent nor benevolent. It is genuinely vital. We become witnesses to the creative and the procreative impulse, a raw and inspiring spectacle.

In an era where food is processed, employment is bureaucratized, entertainment is institutionalized, and education is pre-programmed, we as humans have grown disconnected from our original vitalizing forces. Harrison provides the means for us to reunite with our animal ancestors. Creepers, crawlers, soarers, and swimmers lead us back to the frontier. And we begin anew.

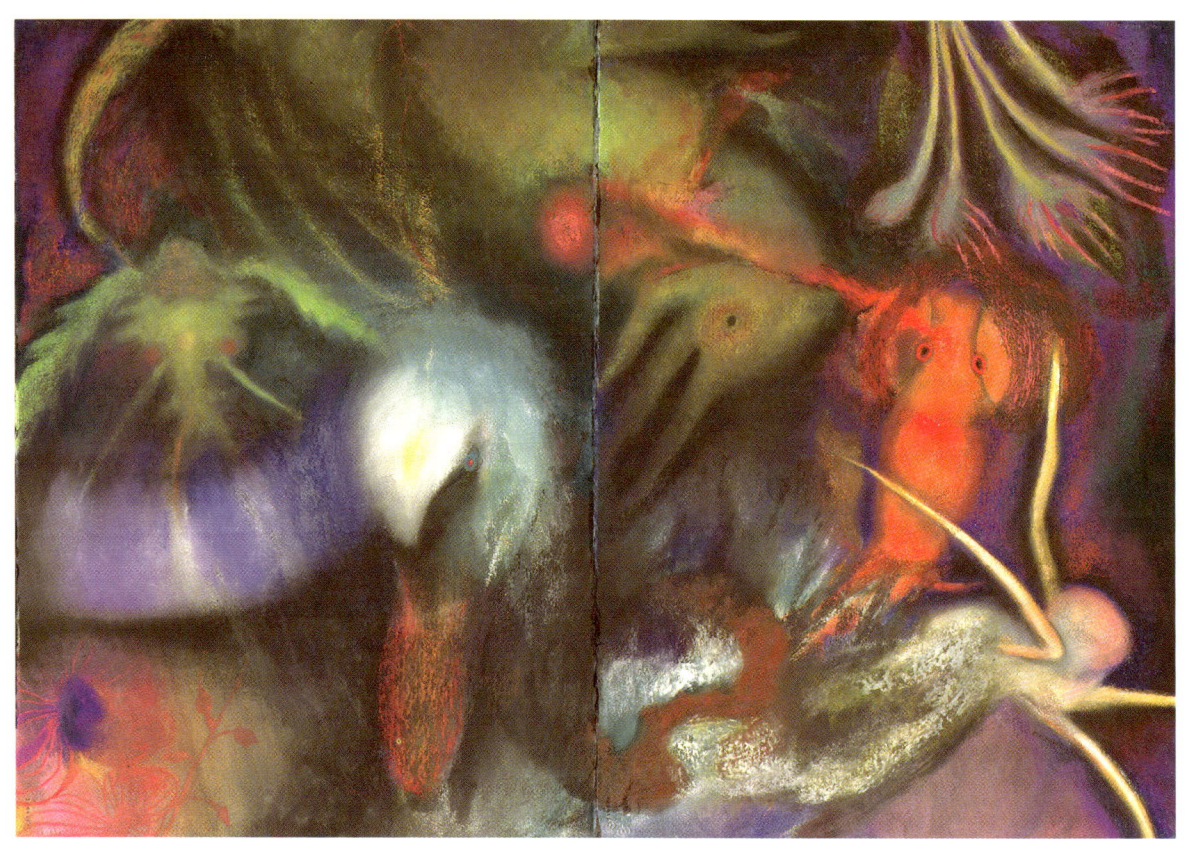

WATER PULSE
2000
pastel, charcoal and oilstick on rag paper
30¹⁄₄ x 44¹⁄₂ inches
(diptych)

Monsters! Their rude and barbarous forms crawled up columns, crept along balustrades, and hung from the balconies of church architecture. Ancient manuscripts are strewn with their tormenting guises. As evil incarnate, they reminded sinners of the tribulations that awaited them, whether in the eternal afterlife or in the days to come.

Today, monsters populate Hollywood horror films, action comic books, and fantastical literature, animation, and children's toys. In these ways, monsters have perpetuated their linguistic root across these vast spans of time; "monstrum" not only means a divine omen, it indicates a misfortune of divine proportions. Monsters violate the natural order. They sprout demonic appendages or fuse limbs from incongruous species. These creatures are conjured by the human imagination to stir fear and loathing.

The figures inhabiting Jan Harrison's work conform to the physical definition of monsters, but, remarkably, they do not seem to generate anguish or grief. Her amphibian/mammal/reptilian/bird convergences are not grotesque; their anatomical distortions are not horrifying; and their unearthly facial demeanors are not repulsive. Their curious impact reflects the artist's own relationship to her images. She describes them as "a treasure, a deity within me, a divine thing."

The dark underworld of her imagination is the origin of these crossed-species and merged-biologies. She excavates the arcane kingdom of the human psyche, so long tyrannized by the repressive and oppressive forces of socialization. This psychic zone is located as far from the perceptual faculties of the human organism as from its spiritual affinity to otherworldliness. Furthermore, it exists beyond the reach of personal or behaviorist impulses. Harrison's journey into deep imagination connects her to the million-year history of the human race. The destination of her travels is the animal soul. Her goal is to recover wisdom that was lost in the rush to civilize, to manufacture, and to manage our world.

In Harrison's life, this great mythic leap originates in ordinary, domestic animal experiences—a goldfish living in a glass bowl on her kitchen counter, pet cats scurrying through her house, a vacation swim with a dolphin, a trip to the aquarium. Harrison's experiences are typical. But the ordinariness of her real-life animal contacts yield a startling revelation: if pets and zoos catapult this artist's consciousness into untamed and untrammeled domains, perhaps the imprint of animal awareness is present in all of us.

Her work actualizes and elaborates this proposition. "Real primitive animals are still within us. Bird-fish, aquatic-mammals are in our bodies and minds. They are not invented. I feel it is my work to bring this out."

In determined increments, Harrison penetrates the subconscious and summons the amorphous life forms lurking there. They interweave and dissolve in her vision. Harrison's own likeness serves as a point of departure for this exploration. She initiates each work by creating a conventional portrait in which her body and her humanness appear intact. These borders gradually erode during the prolonged process of working and reworking that ensues. Snake-like, cat-like, fish-like "animoids" emerge. They crawl upon her naked form or perch on her head, wrap themselves across her shoulders or merge their faces into hers. A woman/animal intimacy develops as the work progresses. The work resonates with erotic energies. These erupting figures bite and claw at her until boundaries between flesh, fur, feather, and fin disintegrate. In some works, her body and face appear swollen, red, and misshapen. In others, her skin turns transparent, revealing intricate networks of veins and arteries that travel up her torso and down her arms. This seething capillary activity parallels the psychic pulsations awakened during the art-making process.

Harrison's images do not illustrate specific myths. They serve no narrative and belong to no predetermined context. Instead, retrieving the pure images of primeval consciousness has allowed her to encounter the origins of awareness which she identifies as the ego, love, fear of death, and the merging of knowledge and innocence. Although each of these perceptions may seem exclusively human, her work attests to the fact that they derive from the ancestors who predate our human relatives—the animals. The animal soul conveys our ingredients of awareness in their elemental form: ego, love, death, and knowledge.

Harrison has noted that egocentricity seems to prevail throughout our culture. Most often, our judgements are based on subjectivity. We value those things that benefit us and provide personal life-enhancement. She then comments: "This narcissism extends beyond an obsession with the self. It also appears as towering urban architecture and disregard for the environment. The ego drives us to aspire to reach the top of a pinnacle. It hinders us as humans. It makes us unable to love."

In re-imagining and re-animating the animal soul, Harrison accomplishes two ego-defying feats that serve herself and her viewers. First, she envisions animal consciousness in which need does not exceed necessity. Second, she connects to the transpersonal world of myth, demonstrating that restoring our animal soul can only be accomplished if we transcend our human ego.

Harrison does not idealize animals. She states: "Animals are capable of cruelty and tenderness. They display both the vileness and the divine beauty in the universe. They manifest the two sides of love." How can vileness be conceived of as an aspect of love? She explains: "Animals may be cunning and they may murder, but the aggression they display involves an acceptance of change that is inherent to the life force. There is a form of human aggression which is of a different order. It attempts to suppress the life force. Destructive aggression stems from fear of growth and change. This desire makes us stiff, like cardboard. I want to be soft and round."

Thus, Harrison suggests, animals do not protest lapses of altruism, the inevitability of suffering, and the inescapable tragedy inherent in the life force. Their engagement in the world is all-inclusive. This life-affirming spirit is the force of love.

As in all-encompassing love, so it is in regard to death that the animal soul is distinguished from human awareness. In fact, the inclinations of today's populace regarding death hardly justifies the use of the word "awareness." Most people avoid attending to death. Their last moments are spent in the antiseptic, impersonal environment of a hospital or nursing home. Harrison proposes: "We fear death because we perceive everything related to our personal egos. Even our dying is narcissistic. People have lost their connection to death and the underworld." Unlike humans, animals are not afflicted with the dread of death. They belong to nature's cycle of birth, death, and rebirth. In dying, animals return home. They offer solace to humans who resist their status as mortals.

Harrison seeks a synthesis of our dualities. We are part male and part female, human and animal, predator and prey, living and dying, brutal and calm, knowledgeable and innocent. "I feel like someone took a cleaver and separated the two sides. It is because the force of sexuality and the inevitability of death are so feared. Art can reunite us. I am working for my character, working to become whole, an authentic person, not just an artist."

Besides articulating this theme in her visual work, Harrison has literally enacted the two voices that she discovered in her childhood fantasies when she conjured two fictional playmates. One was dark, powerful, and wild. The other was shy, responsible, and modest. The two struggled to become integrated.

Harrison describes the strange, preverbal language that she utters as an animal tongue, although it does not imitate the sounds made by any known animals. Like her visual art, this language displays evidence of a deep imaginative reality. It extends the maxim ascribed by Carl Jung that the soul is primarily a repository of images. Here the soul is also a repository of languages. In Harrison's work, both reconnect her with the archaic moorings of our shared precivilized natures.

Harrison's animal speech consists of two voices. One is dark and all-encompassing. The other is child-like and high pitched. It pleads with the dark power, "Please don't make me have to die." This is the cry of innocence confronting knowledge. It epitomizes the search to unify the demands of the soul with the mechanisms of survival.

This dialogue positions the artist within a flow that lies outside of linear thinking and measured time progression. It allows the artist to exist in the manner of an animal. "When I am speaking in animal tongues, I close off a part of my brain. Then I can interact with the part that I find in animals and some human beings. It is more unified."

Although they are innocent of their roles as teachers, animals show us a way to be released from the weight of the human experience and enjoy an encompassing harmony. This is because they are exempt from the alienating forces of encoded language and externally-imposed patterns of behavior. Harrison seeks this release through her creative process, and she offers it to viewers who experience its outcomes.

L.W. 1998

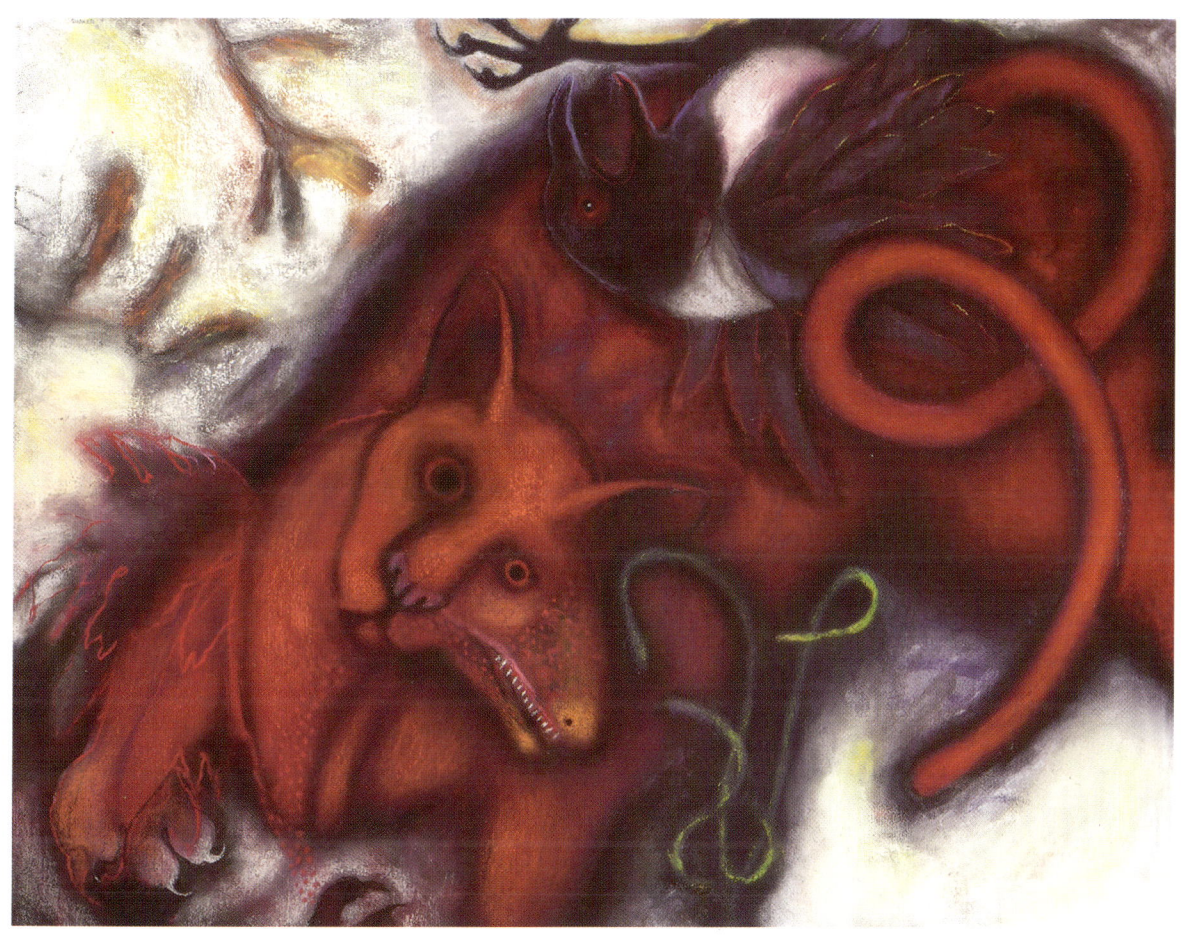

SHAKER
1999
pastel and oilstick on lavis fidelis paper
34 ³/₁₆ x 45¹/₄ inches

As Long as I Can Remember

As long as I can remember I have loved animals and felt a kinship with them. But loving animals is not the same thing as accepting the power and vulnerability of the life force within ourselves and within the world. My work is concerned with the paradox of the power of nature with regard to our own sense of order or justice. Through communion with the animal nature, linking instinct and intellect, the dualities of knowledge and innocence, power and weakness, sacred and profane, show themselves as two sides of the psyche of the world.

Coming from a personal and universal myth which faces joy and suffering, selflessness and narcissism, my work reflects the part of ourselves, and of the world, that is both all-encompassing and molecular. In addition to painting and sculpture, I speak in a language, "Animal Tongue," which acts as an avenue or bridge to the world beneath the surface, and enables me to live and see clearly.

Originating from a love of the life force, my work finds a connection between the "reptilian brain" and altruism. Occurring from a place similar to dreams, and acted out within an inner landscape, the images reestablish a link with the wonder and mystery of the life force.

Jan Harrison
January 1, 2001

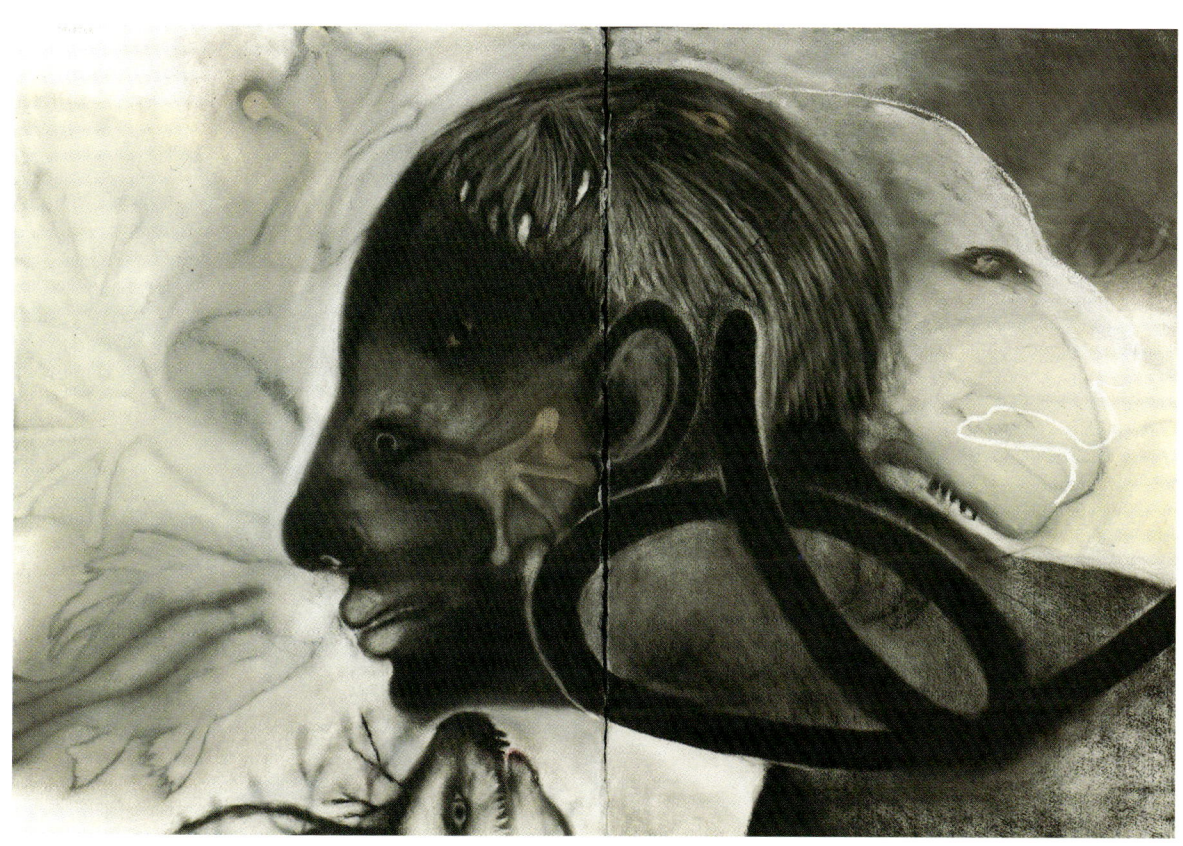

TWISTER
1996
charcoal, pastel and gouache on rag paper
30¹/₄ x 44¹/₂ inches
(diptych)

JAN HARRISON 13

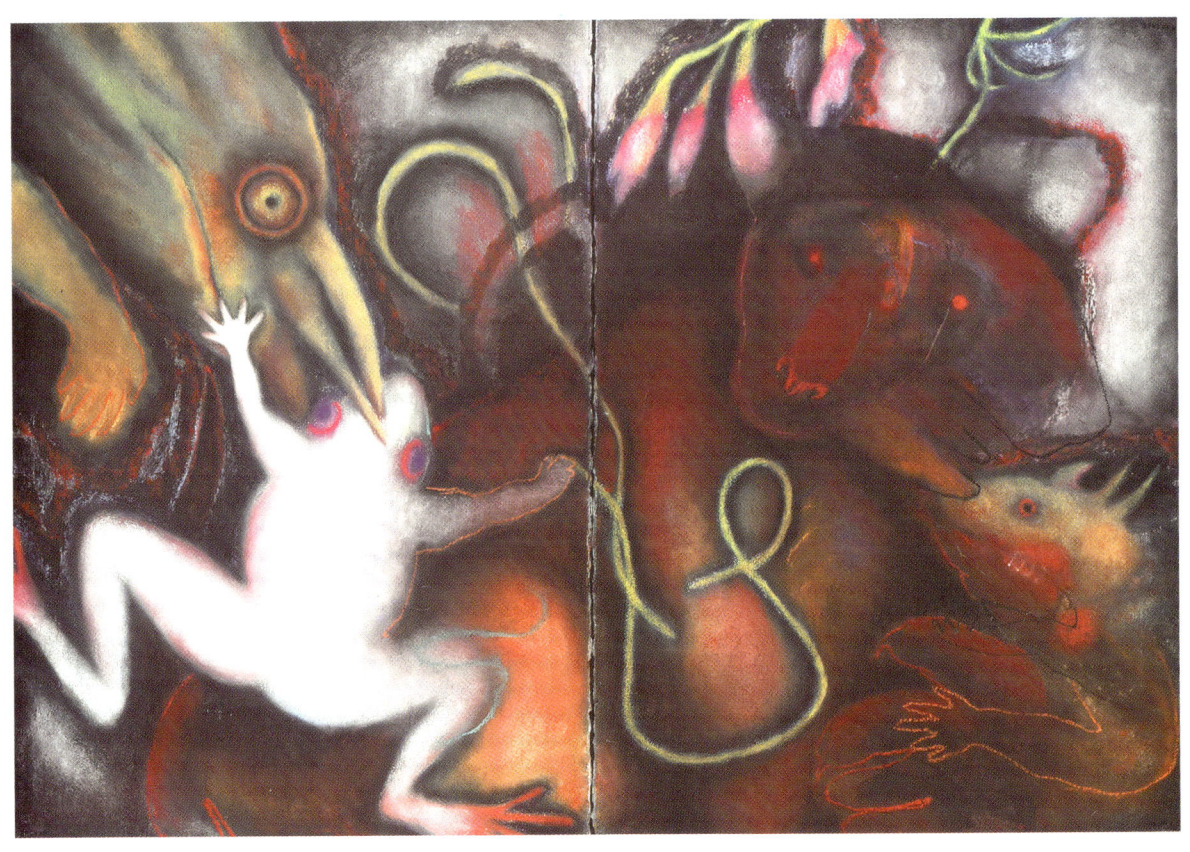

LEPORATA
1999
pastel, charcoal and oilstick on rag paper
30 1⁄4 x 44 1⁄2 inches
(diptych)

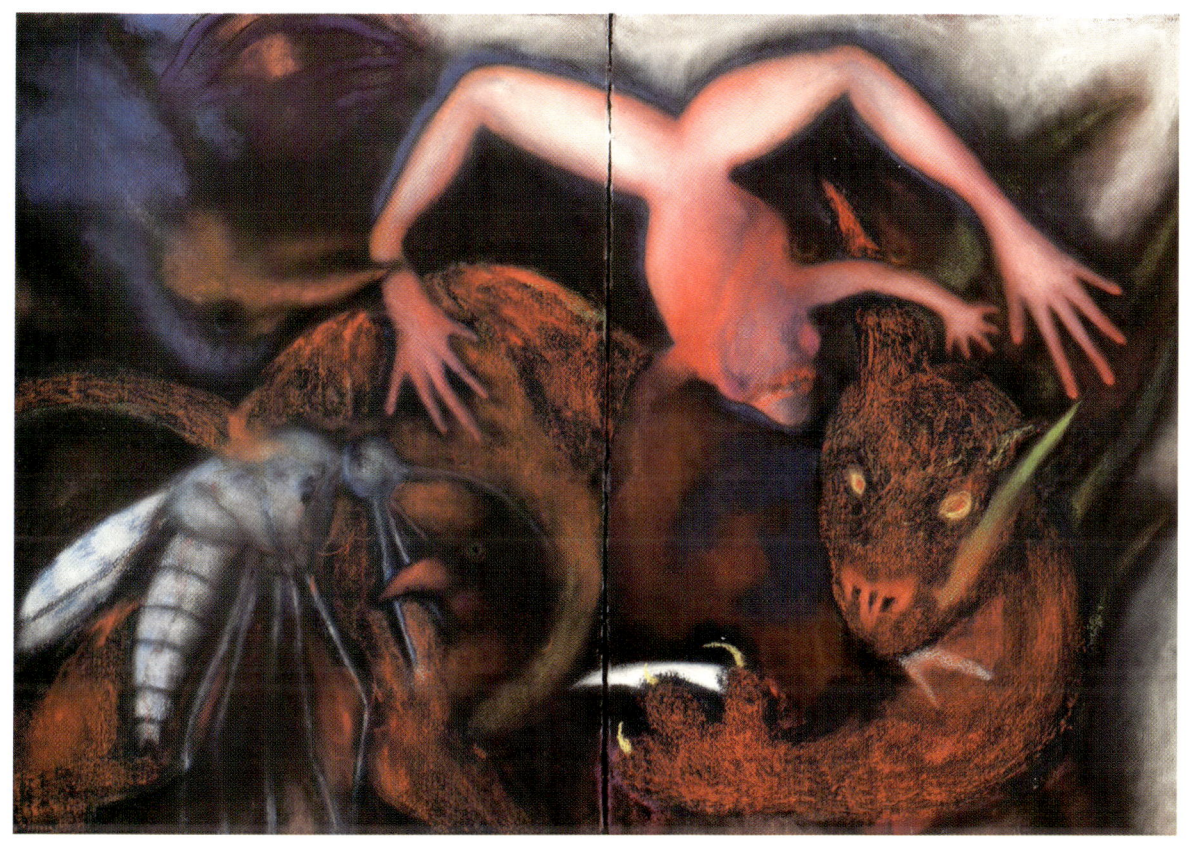

GERONCIA
1999
pastel, charcoal and oilstick on rag paper
$30^{1}/_{4}$ x $44^{1}/_{2}$ *inches*
(diptych)

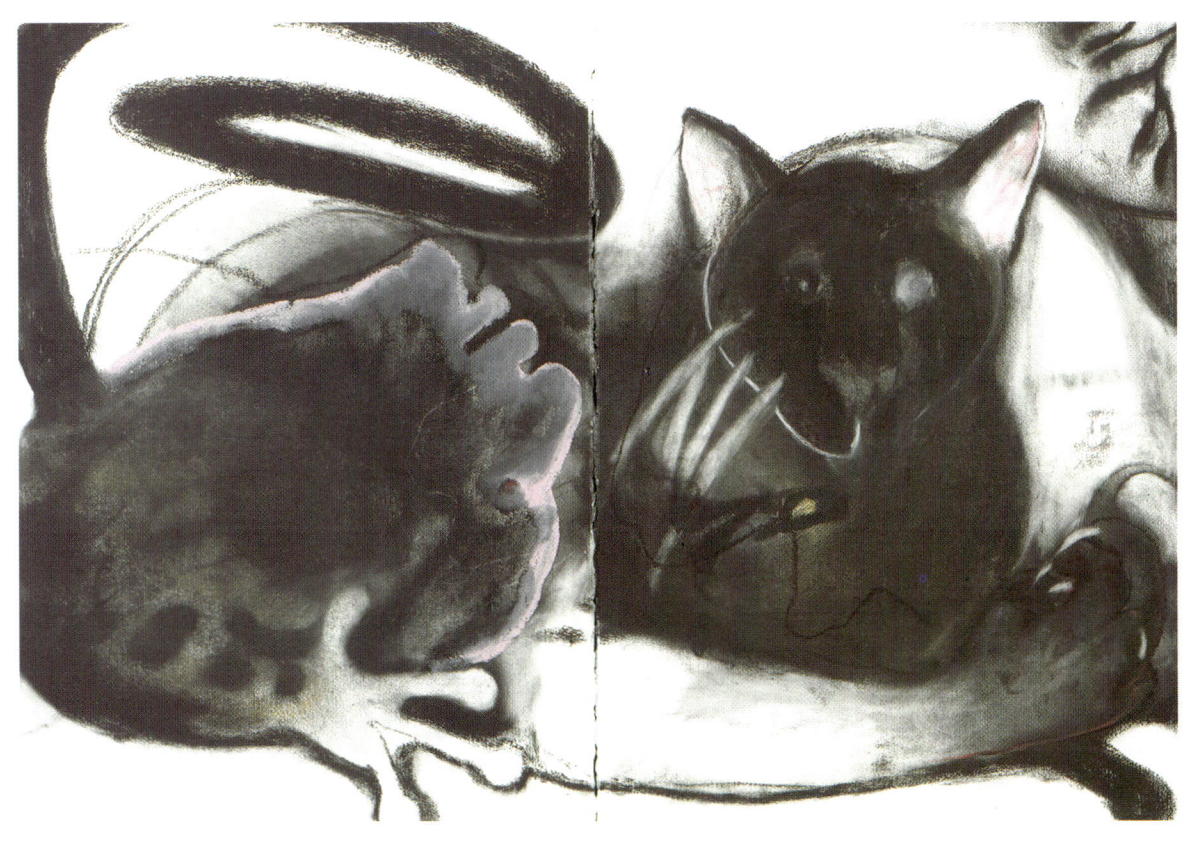

SPOT ON TEMPLE
1996
charcoal, pastel and oilstick on rag paper
30 1/4 x 44 1/2 inches
(diptych)

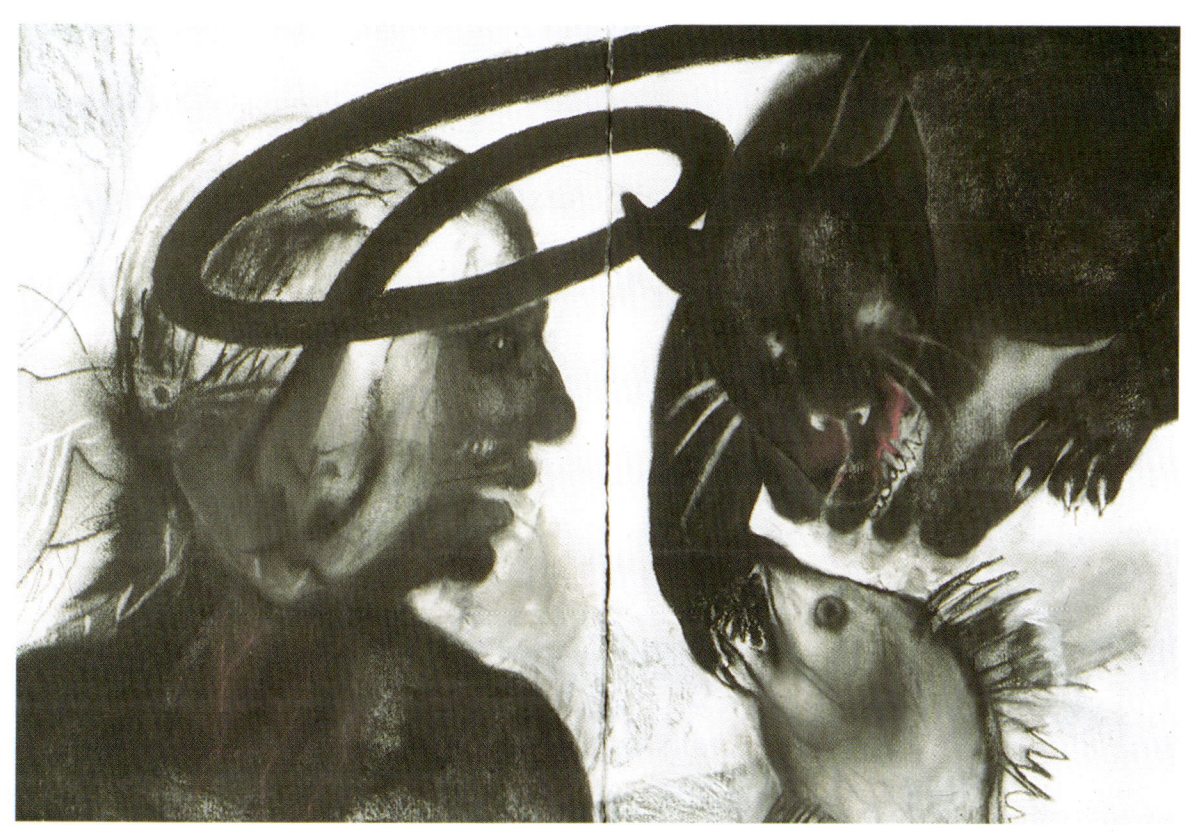

Now You See Me
1996
charcoal, pastel and gouache on rag paper
30¹/₄ x 44¹/₂ inches
(diptych)

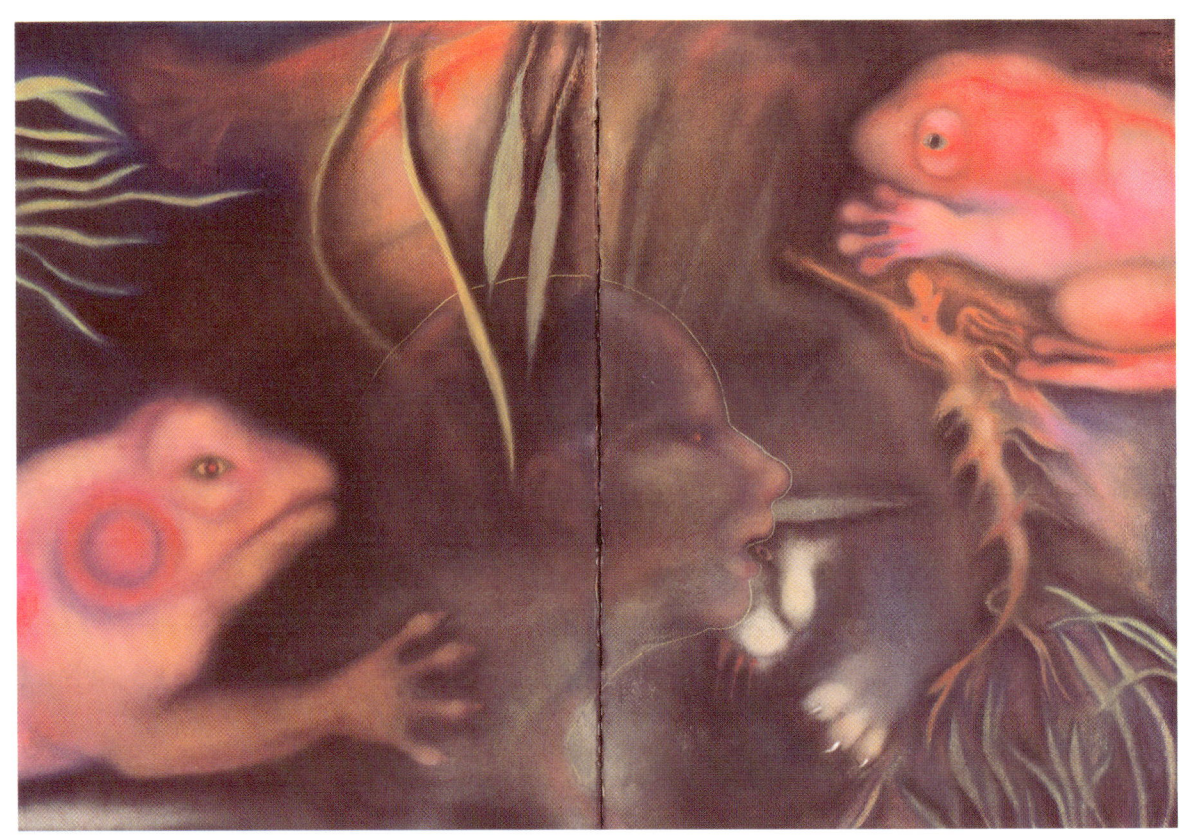

LEAP CHING
1997
pastel on rag paper
30 1/4 x 44 1/2 inches
(diptych)

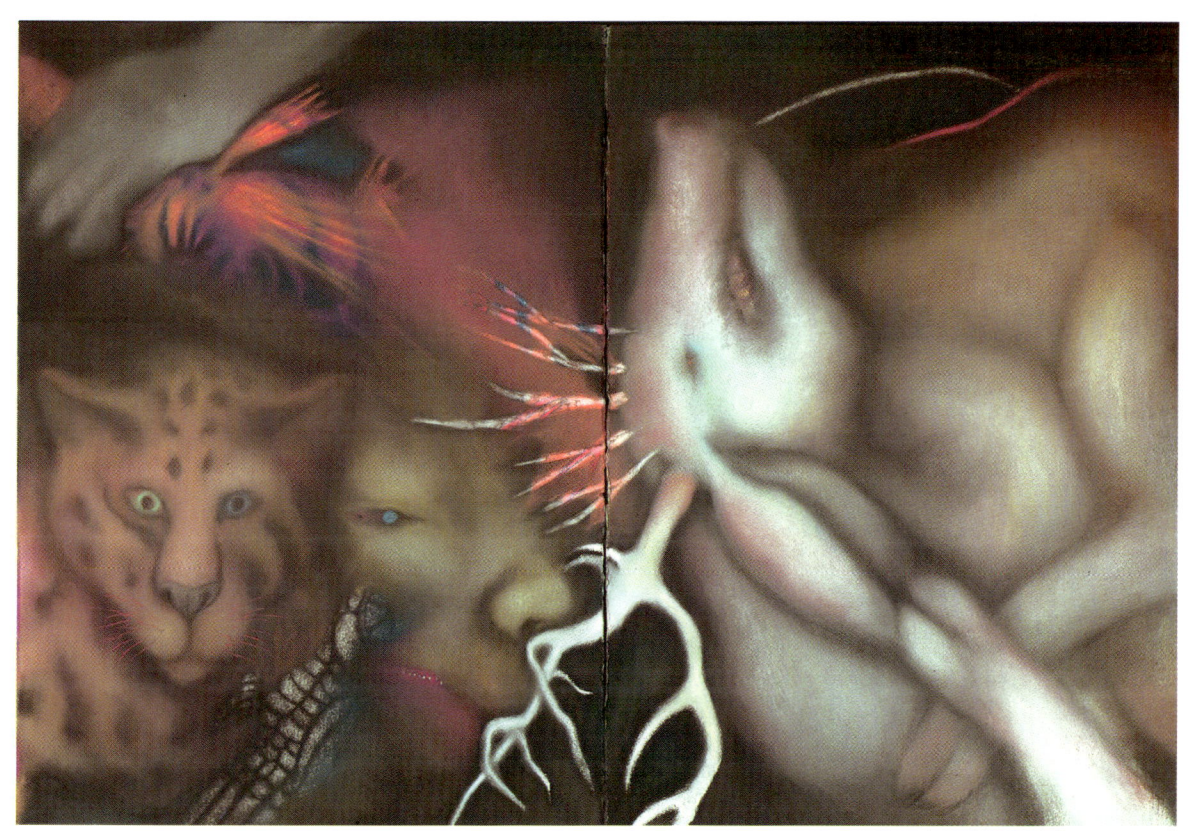

CHUFF AND ROLL OVER
1997
pastel on rag paper
30 1/4 x 44 1/2 inches
(diptych)

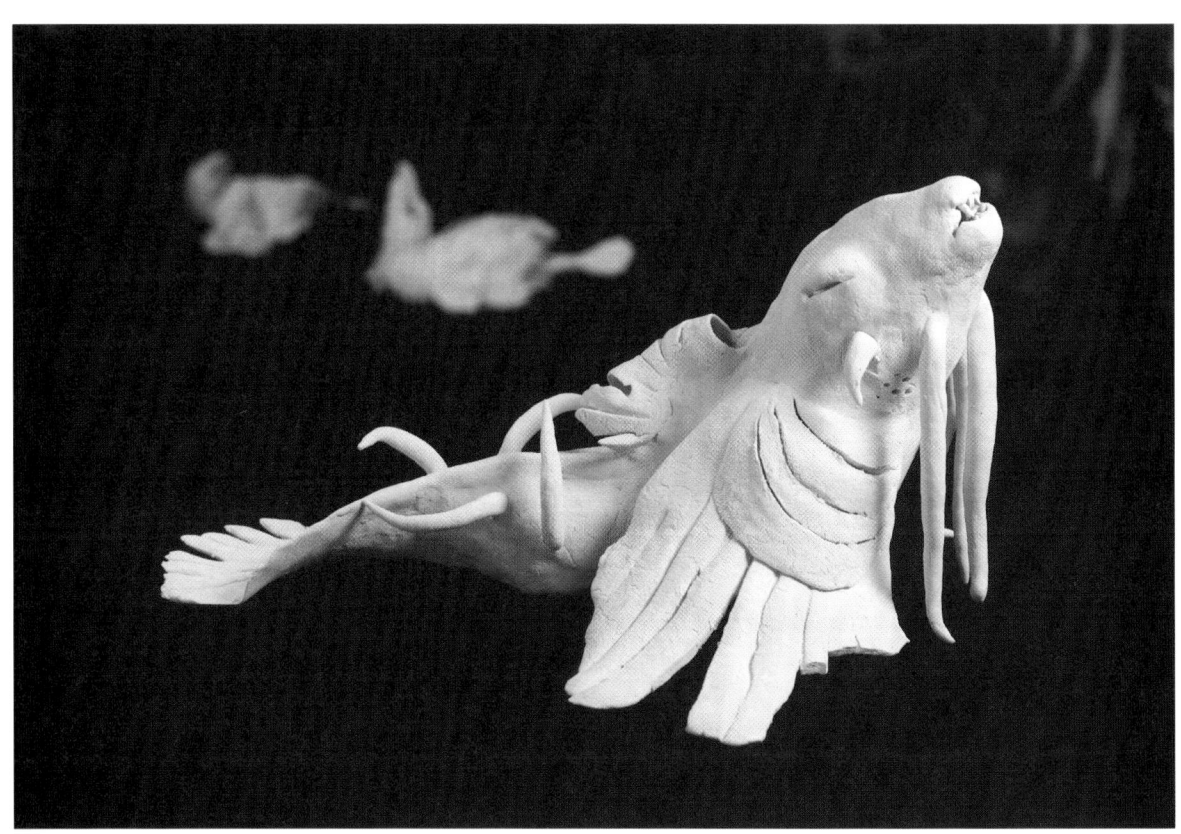

TENDRIL BIRDFISH
1997
bisque-fired porcelain
19 x 15½ x 9¼ inches

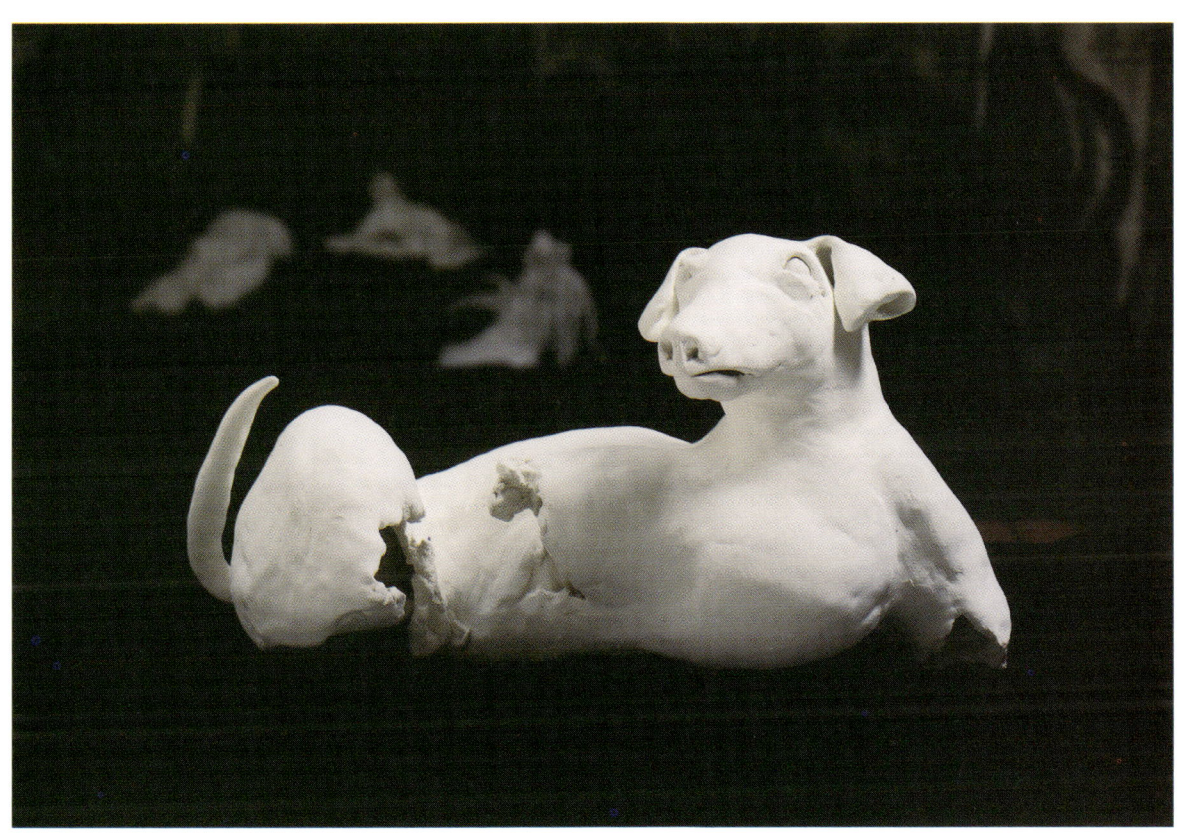

DOG WITH NO LEGS
1997
bisque-fired porcelain
19 x 9¹/₄ x 9¹/₄ inches

Jan Harrison began speaking in Animal Tongues in 1979, after completing *The Tongue Drawing*, which was on tongue-shaped pieces of paper, waterproofed, and attached to a drinking water fountain. The viewer could drink the water, which would flow down the drawing.

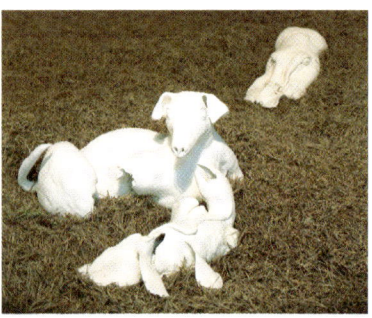

ANIMAL TONGUES
1998 Installation
Detail from exhibition. ANIMAL, ANIMA, ANIMUS,
Pori Art Museum, Pori, Finland
porcelain sculptures, pine needles,
and Animal Tongue audiotape,
including tongue spoken by the artist
with animal sounds

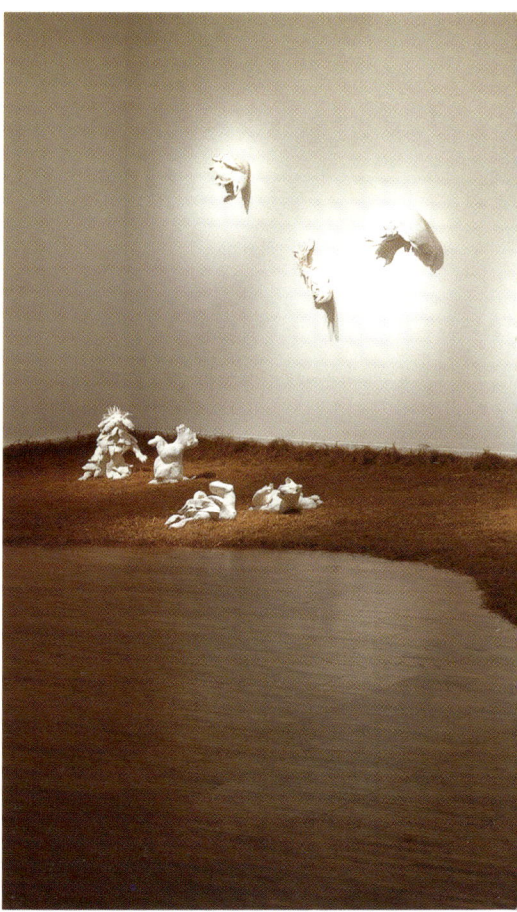

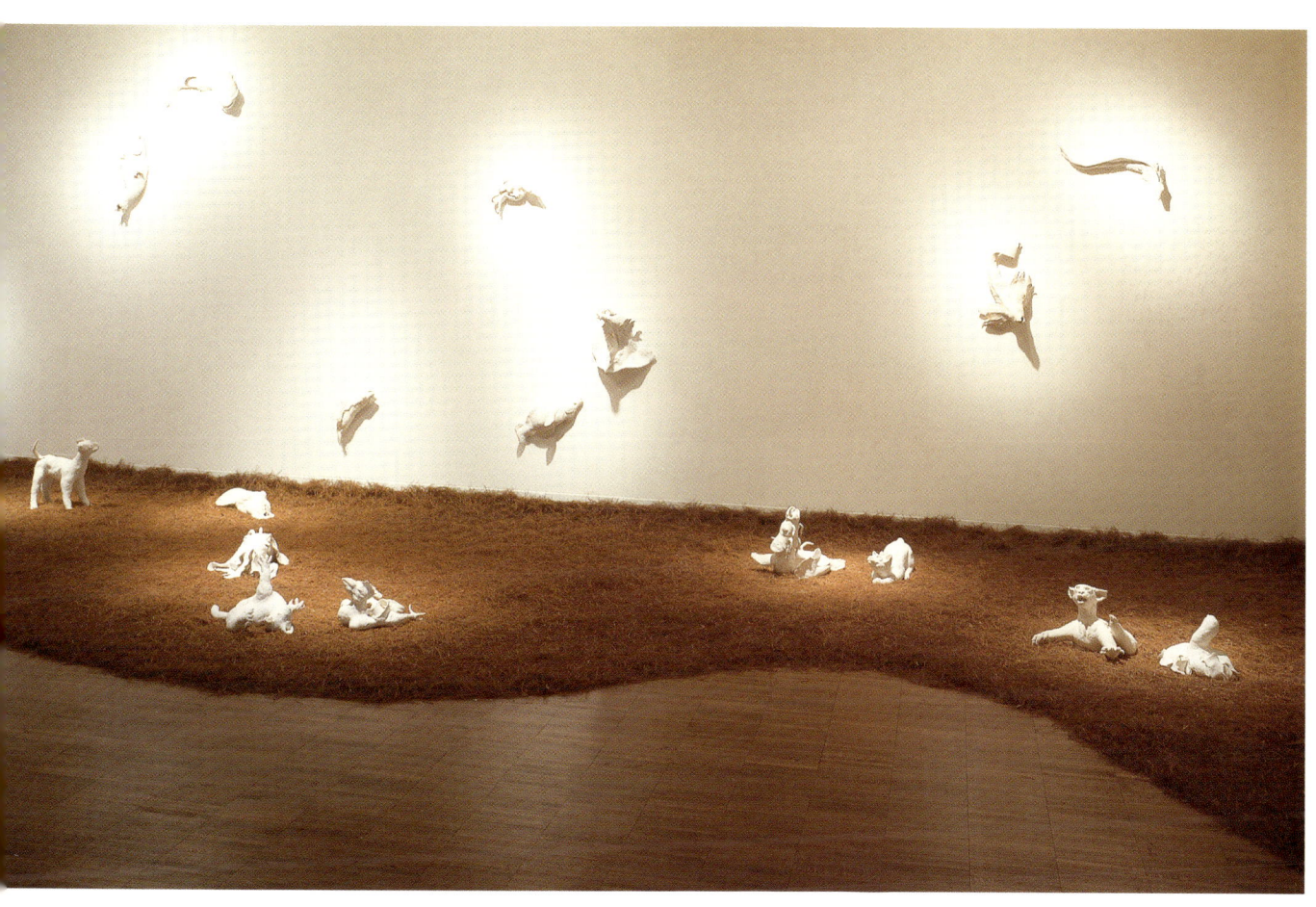

ANIMAL TONGUES
1999 Installation
From exhibition, ARCANA MUNDI,
Alice F. and Harris K. Weston Art Gallery
Aronoff Center for the Arts, Cincinnati, Ohio
15 x 37 feet
bisque-fired porcelain, pine needles, and Animal Tongue audiotape

ANIMAL LOVE TRANSCENDS
THE LIMITS OF MALE AND FEMALE.
THE ANIMAL HAS A CLUMSY GRACE,
NOT TO BE WORSHIPPED
AS AN ENTITY.

1980 journal entry

animal wishes/animal desires   My tongue has nostrils.

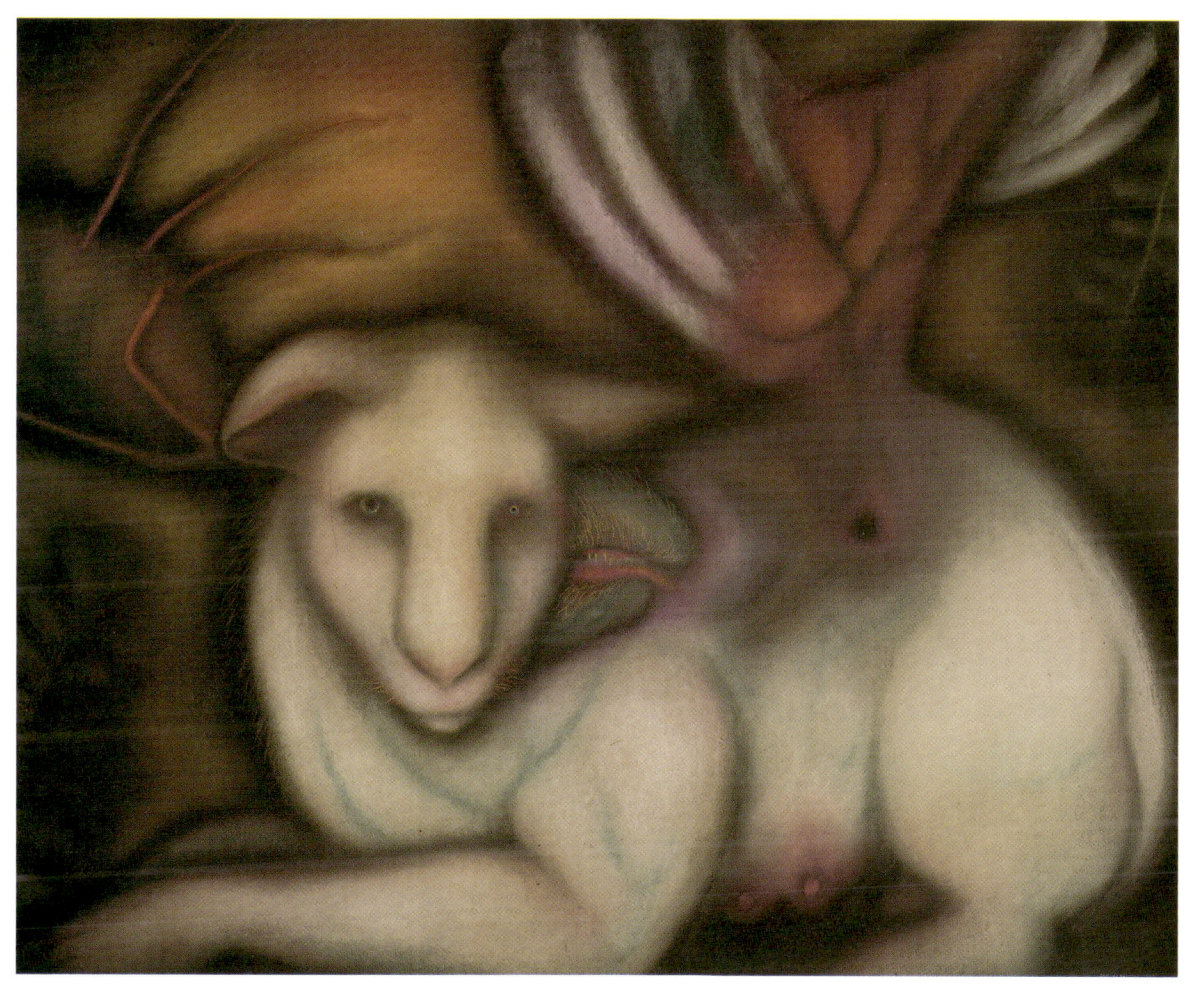

APOTHEO
1993
pastel and colorpencil on lavis fidelis
45 ^{1}⁄$_4$ x 34 ^{3}⁄$_{16}$ inches

CONCERNING TIME AND THE DYING ANIMAL

MY CAT IS DYING, OF CANCER, BUT DYING WITH
THE GRACE OF THE ACCEPTANCE OF THE
WAY IT MUST BE. HE IS VERY SELF-CONTAINED,
ALTHOUGH HIS BODY IS BONY, AND HE SMELLS
LIKE HE IS SICK. A MINUTE TO HIM SEEMS TO
BE AN ETERNITY AND A SECOND AT THE
SAME TIME. THIS WAS TRUE IN HEALTH AS
WELL AS SICKNESS. HE KNOWS WHAT IT MEANS
TO LIVE FOREVER, BECAUSE HE DOES NOT
MEASURE TIME IN MINUTES, HOURS, DAYS
OR YEARS. HE KNOWS TIME AS A CONTINUUM,
ALL TOGETHER.

1985 journal entry

the tiny voice   *It sings to the ecstatic cells....and the tired cells bark right back.*

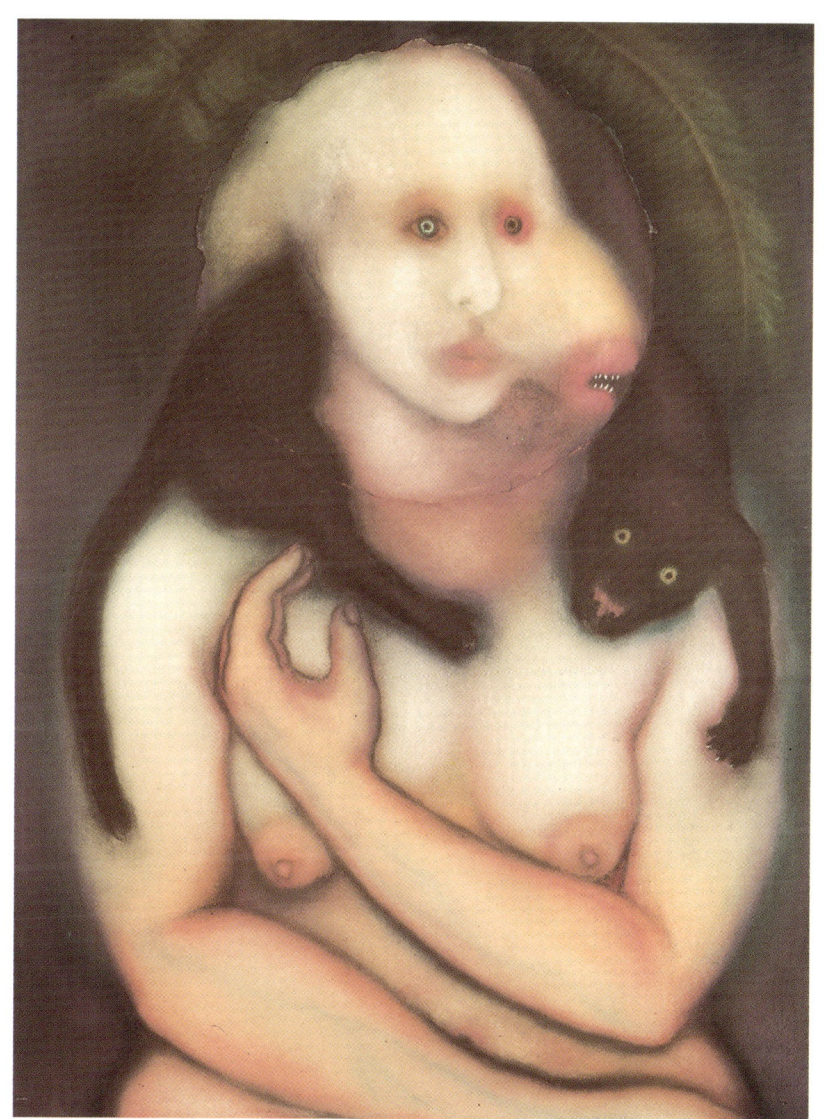

MAMARYE
1992
pastel collage on rag paper
30 1/4 x 22 1/4 inches
Collection of the artist

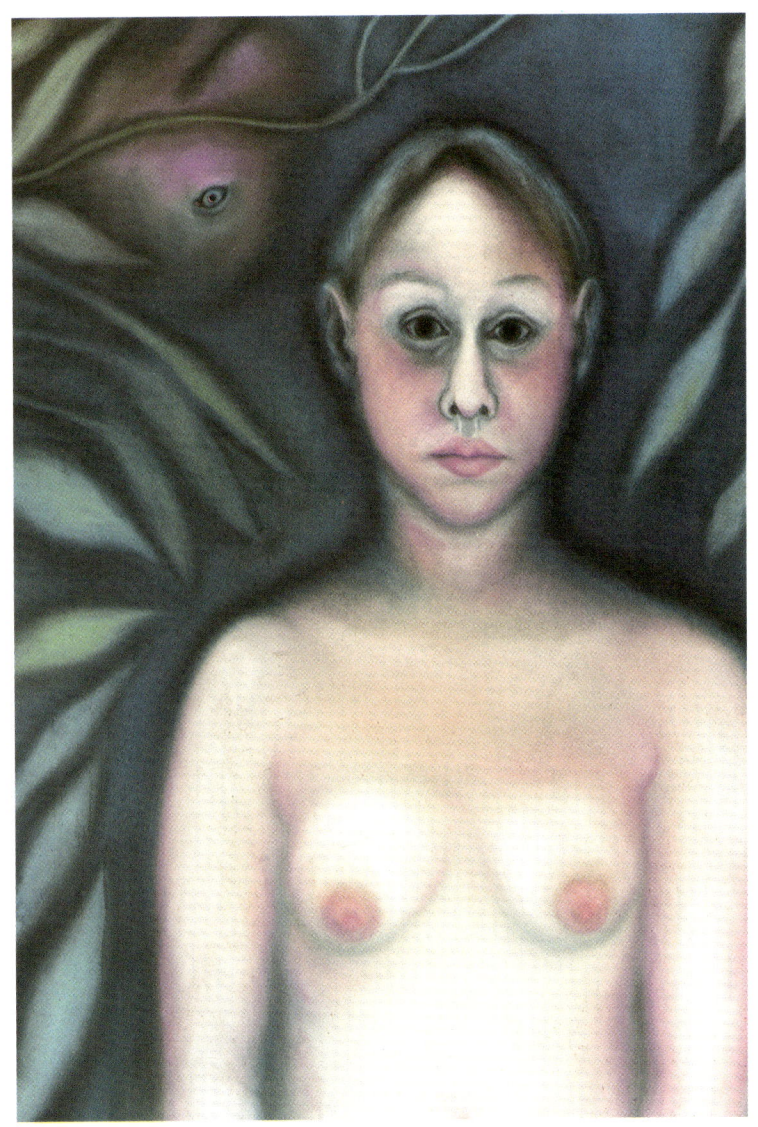

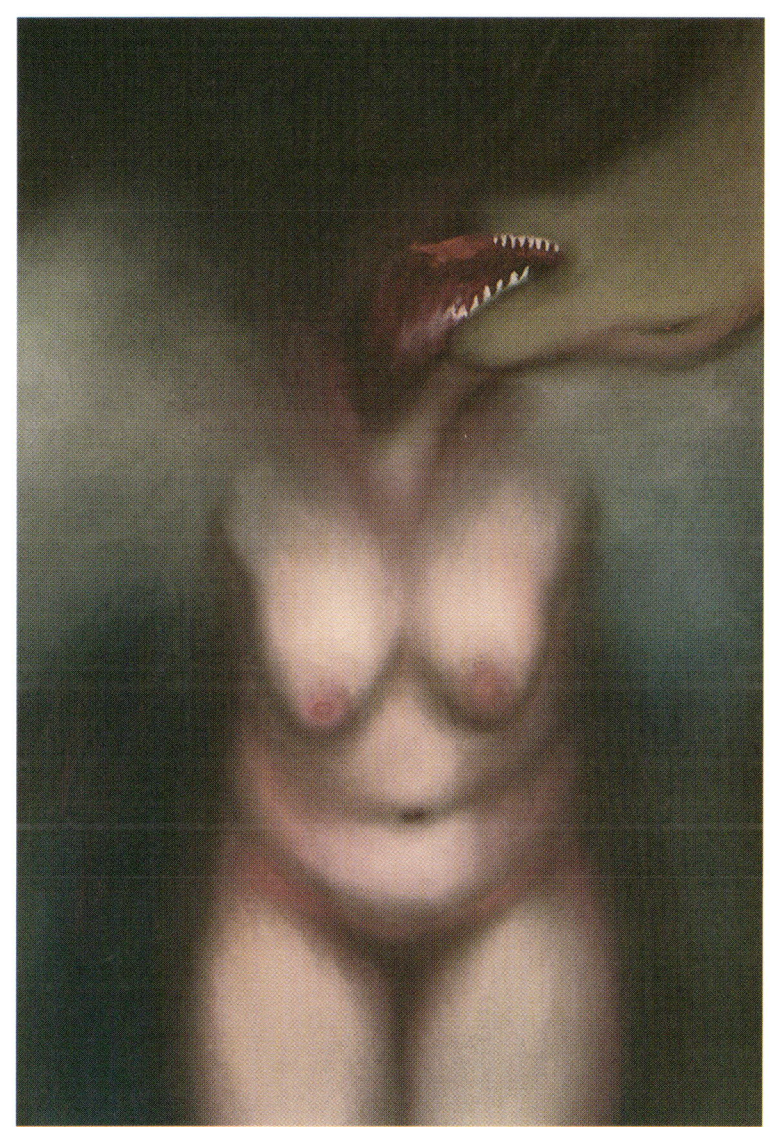

THE BARGAIN
The Expulsion Series, 1987
pastel and colorpencil on rag paper
44 ¹/₂ x 30 inches

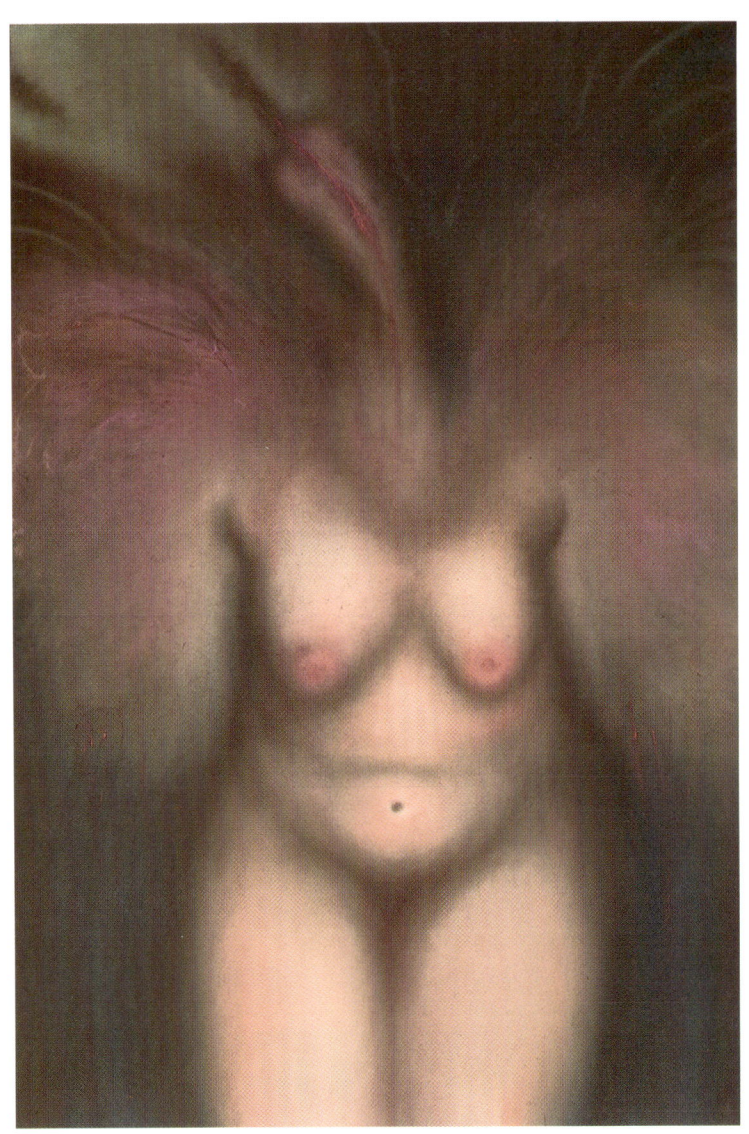

THE KISS
The Expulsion Series, 1987
pastel and colorpencil on rag paper
44 1/2 x 30 inches
Collection: Nancy Moore, New York, NY

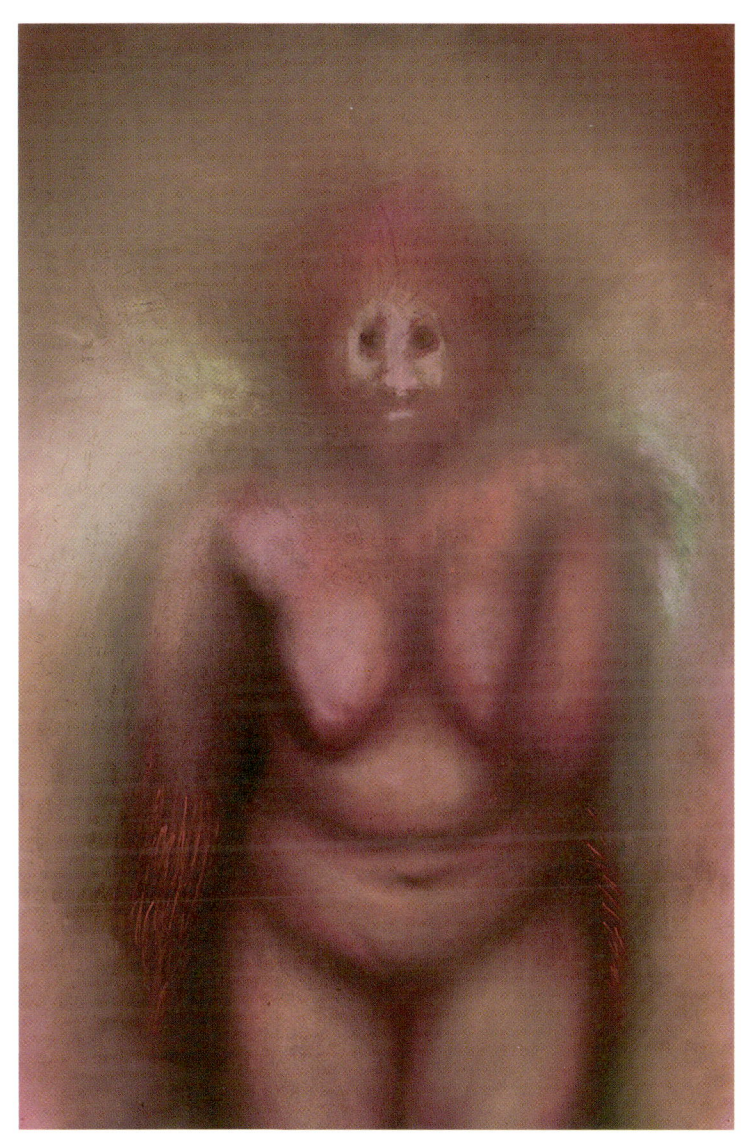

EXPULSION TO ASHES
The Expulsion Series, 1987
pastel and colorpencil on rag paper
44 1/2 x 30 inches

ANCIENT NEWS

ABOUT A MILLION YEARS AGO, CAVE ARTISTS DREW
ANIMALS ON THE WALLS OF CAVES. THE CHEST AND
SINEWS WENT BACK AND FORTH. THERE WAS
GREAT CLUMSY BEAUTY. SOME OF THE RED PIGMENT
WAS BLOOD. SOME OF THE BROWN PIGMENT WAS FECES.
THINGS WERE GLUED ON WITH SPIT. A HUNDRED MILLION
YEARS AGO, WE DID SOMETHING LIKE JUMPING OR
LEAPING, OR FLIPPING OVER. OUR TAILS WORKED LIKE
POLE-VAULTS, TO HELP US OVER HURDLES. WE HAD
OPENINGS AND PROTRUSIONS BETWEEN OUR LEGS, TO
PUT ONE INSIDE THE OTHER PERSON, WHICH FELT
GOOD, AS IT WAS AN EXTENSION OF LOVE. ASIDE
FROM OUR GENITALIA, WE WERE ESSENTIALLY
THE SAME. A HUNDRED ~~~~~~ YEARS AGO,
WHEN WE LICKED OUR COMPANIONS ON THE NECK,
A SMILE CAME UP AROUND OUR MOUTHS.
(NOT OUT THROUGH OUR TEETH, LIKE NOW.)

1981 journal entry

tyrra vas terra

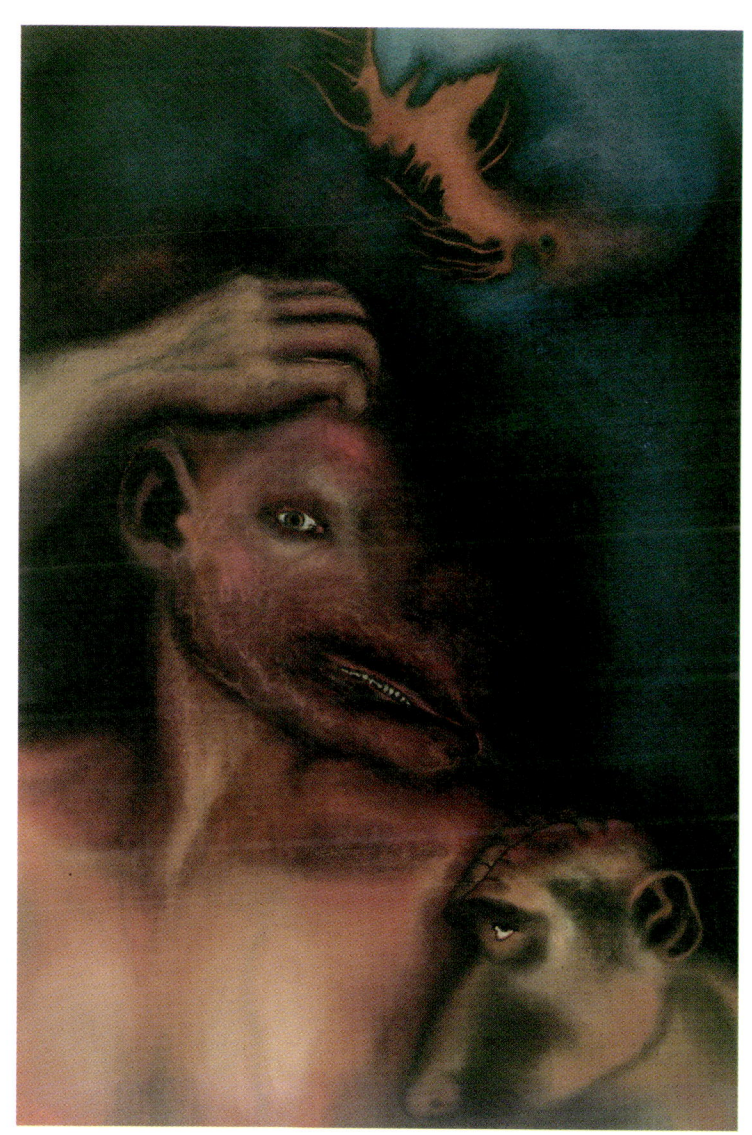

THE DEVIL'S ADVOCATE
A Perilous Eden Series, 1987
pastel and colorpencil on lavis fidelis
52 ¹/₂ x 35 ¹/₂ inches
Collection: Sergiu Luca and Margaret LeCompte,
Boulder, Colorado

I WENT TO A CONFERENCE, AND I WAS NAKED.
ONE WOMAN, WELL DRESSED, SUGGESTED THAT I
PUT SOMETHING ON — BUT I CONDUCTED THE
WORKSHOP NAKED.

1995 dream

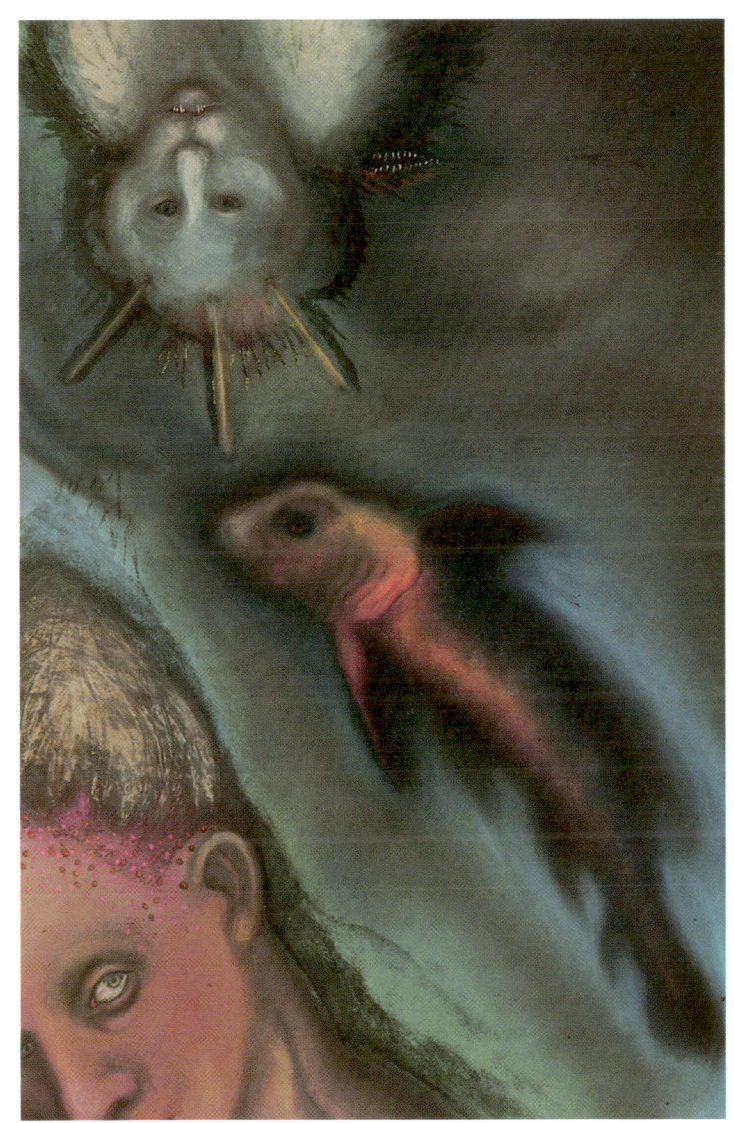

THE EUCHARIST
A Perilous Eden Series, 1988
pastel, colorpencil and oilstick on lavis fidelis
52 1/2 x 35 1/2 inches
Collection: John Henderson and Richard DuBeshter
Chicago, Illinois

BASEBALL GAMES AT NIGHT

WHEN I WAS A CHILD, I WOULD
ATTEND BASEBALL GAMES AT
NIGHT. MY MOTHER WAS THE
SECRETARY FOR THE TEAM
WHILE SITTING IN THE
BLEACHERS, I WOULD WATCH
VARIOUS BASEBALL PLAYERS.
SOME OF THEM WERE NAMED
JESUS, WHICH WAS PRONOUNCED
"HEY ZEUS." THEY WOULD
CHEW AND SPIT, BOWING
DOWN AND AROUND, SWINGING
THEIR ARMS AND SHOULDERS
IN AN ∞ SHAPE,
WITH A HANDFUL OF BATS.

1974 journal entry

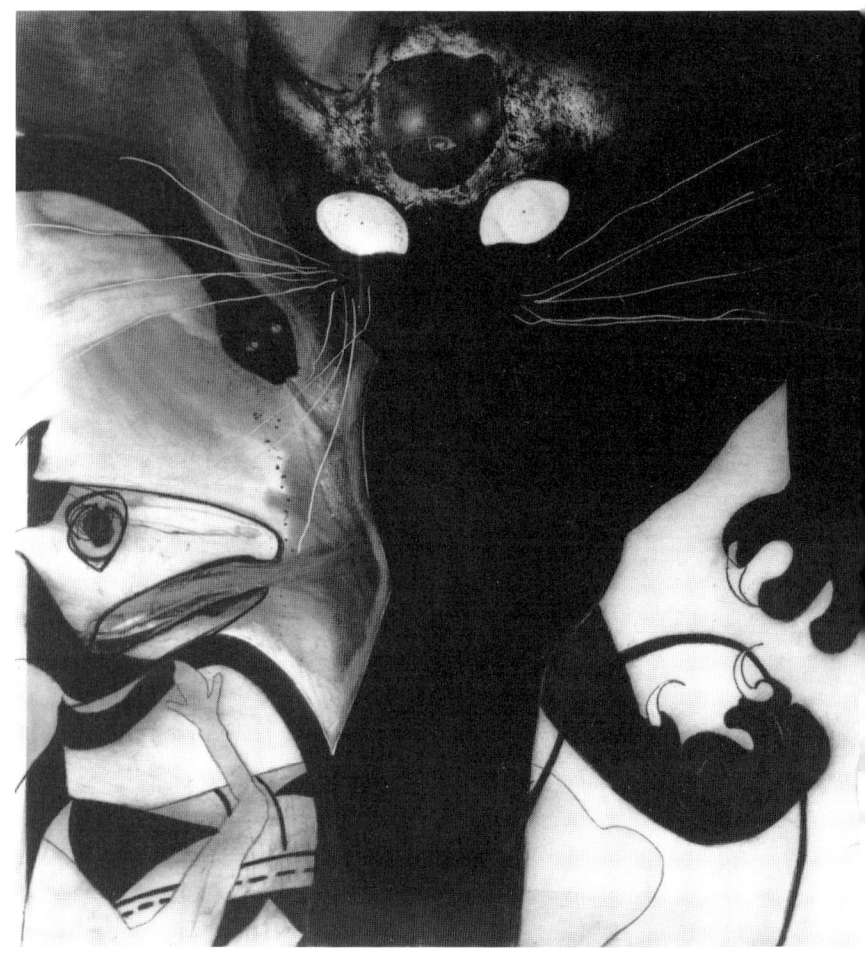

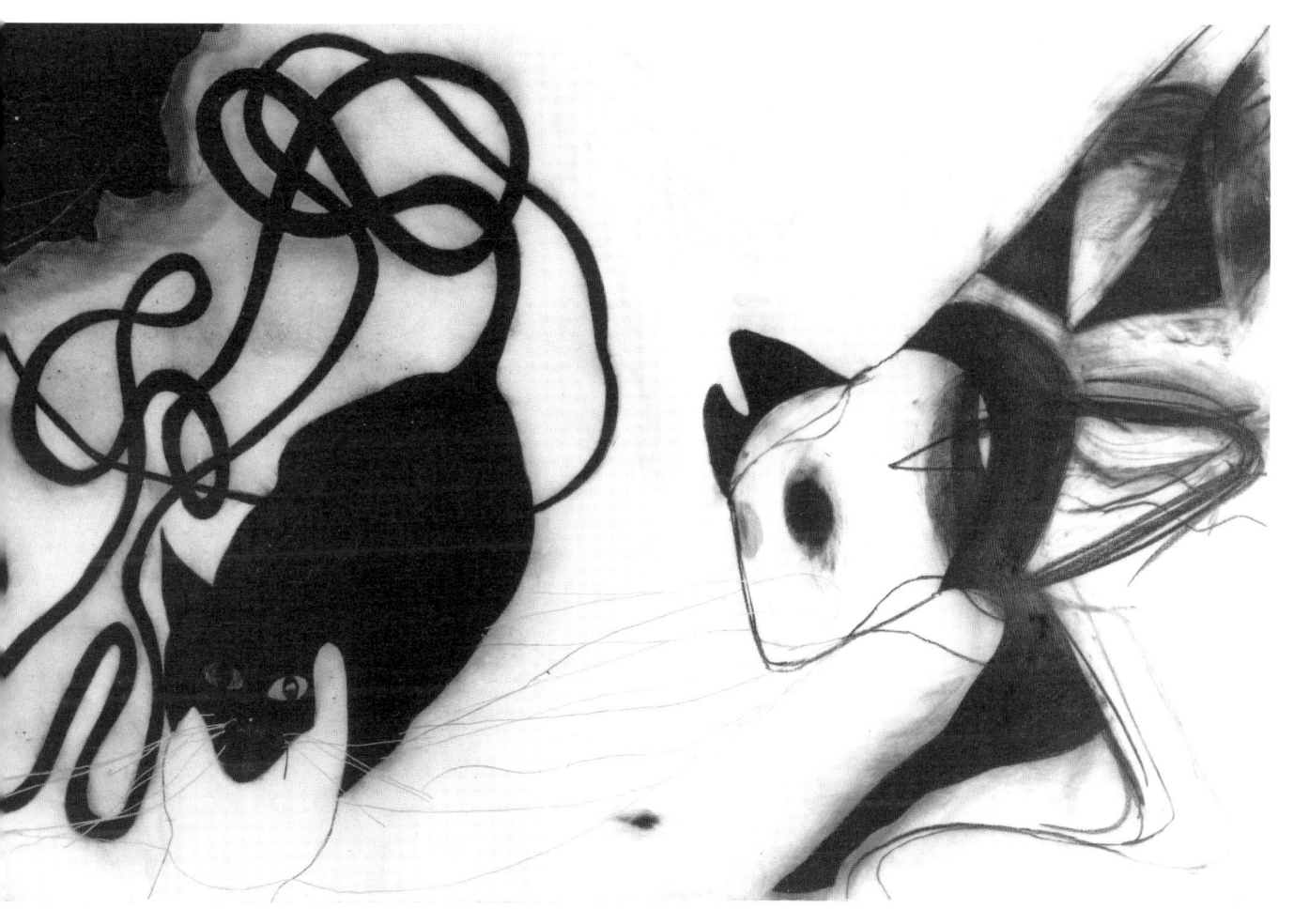

THE ABYSS CROSSING
1980
pastel, charcoal and colorpencil on lavis fidelis
52 1/2 x 131 inches
Collection: The Wexner Center for the Arts, Columbus, Ohio

JAN HARRISON 37

ABOUT THE ARTIST

Jan Harrison was born on December 18, 1944, in West Palm Beach, Florida, the daughter of a railroad telegraph dispatcher and a legal secretary. Raised by her mother and older sister, and left alone for long periods of time, much of her early life was spent with animals. Having previously lived in Georgia, the Mojave Desert, Northern California, and then in Ohio for thirteen years, in 1989 she moved to Ulster County, New York.

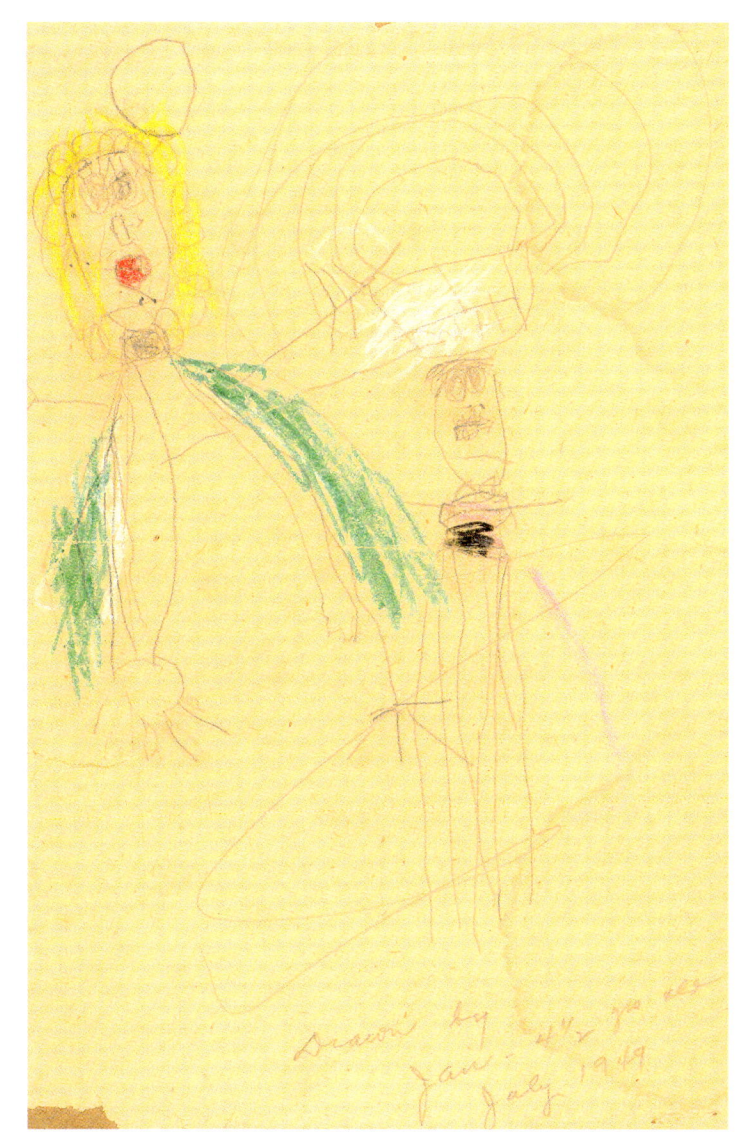

MOTHER AND FATHER
Childhood drawing
1949
crayon and pencil on tablet paper
8 5/16 x 5 1/2 inches

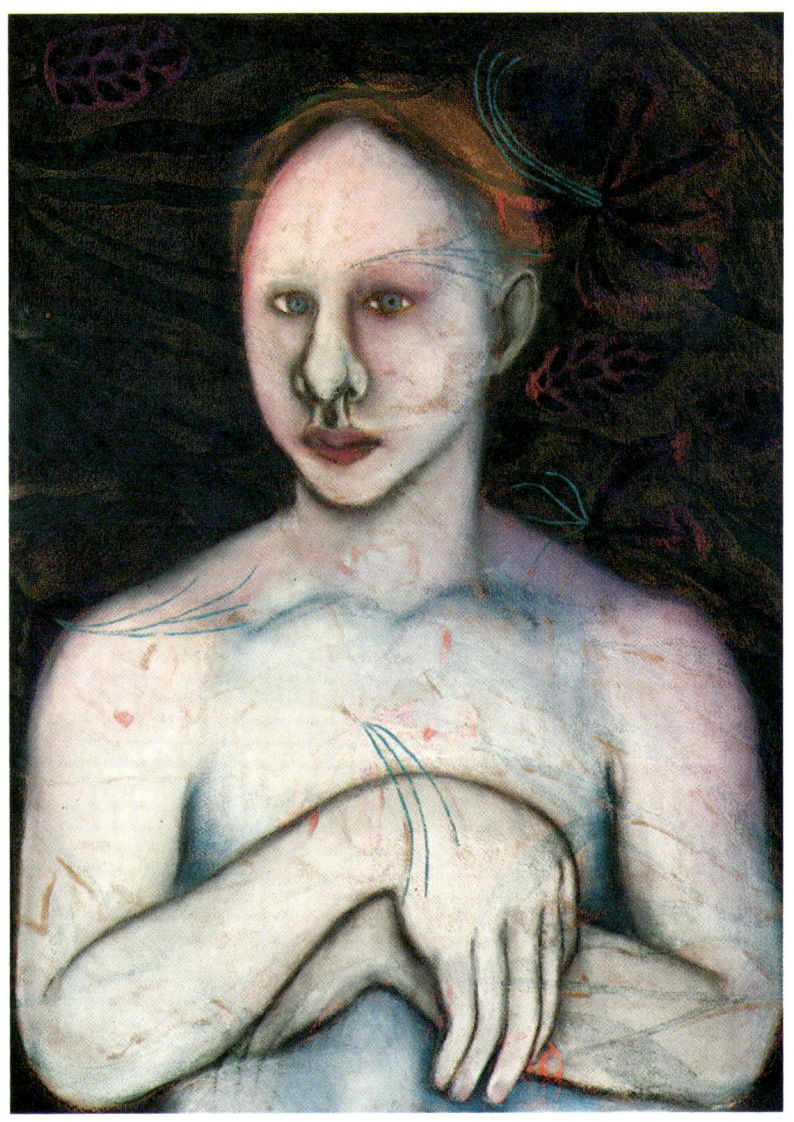

SELF PORTRAIT
WITH FLORAL TATTOOS
1992
pastel and gouache on rag paper
30 1/4 x 22 1/4 inches

SELECTED EXHIBITIONS

Jan Harrison has exhibited in over one hundred solo and group exhibitions. She has produced two house-as-art projects, and has created eight artist's books. Her paintings, drawings, sculptural installations, and audio art have been exhibited throughout the United States and internationally.

2000   *ANIMAL.ANIMA.ANIMUS,* THE WINNIPEG ART GALLERY, Winnipeg, Canada.

1999   *ANIMAL.ANIMA.ANIMUS,* P.S.1 CONTEMPORARY ART CENTER, Long Island City, New York.
ARCANA MUNDI, ALICE F. AND HARRIS K. WESTON ART GALLERY, ARONOFF CENTER FOR THE ARTS, Cincinnati, Ohio. *(solo exhibition)*

1998   *ANIMAL.ANIMA.ANIMUS,* MUSEUM VOOR MODERNE KUNST, Arnhem, Holland.
JAN HARRISON, JAMES YAROSH ASSOCIATES FINE ART, Holmdel, New Jersey. *(solo exhibition)*
ANIMAL.ANIMA.ANIMUS, PORIN TAIDEMUSEO, Pori, Finland.

1997   *IONE'S DREAM FESTIVAL,* THE GALLERY AT THE DEEP LISTENING SPACE, THE PAULINE OLIVEROS FOUNDATION, Kingston, New York.

1996   *ANIMAL CROSSING,* NANCY MOORE FINE ART, New York, New York. *(solo exhibition)*

1995   *BESTIAL ANGELS,* WILLIAM KING REGIONAL ARTS CENTER, Abingdon, Virginia.

1994   *THE DEFINITIVE AMERICAN CONTEMPORARY QUILT,* HOSTRA MUSEUM, Hostra University, Hempstead, New York.

1993   *ANIMAL TONGUES,* WOMEN'S STUDIO WORKSHOP, Rosendale, New York. *(solo exhibition)*
THE DEFINITIVE AMERICAN CONTEMPORARY QUILT, GRAND RAPIDS ART MUSEUM, Grand Rapids, Michigan.
OUTDOOR SCULPTURE, ELENA ZANG GALLERY, Woodstock, New York.

1992   *THE DEFINITIVE AMERICAN CONTEMPORARY QUILT,* WASHINGTON STATE UNIVERSITY MUSEUM OF ART, Pullman, Washington.
TYRRA VAS TERRA, DONSKOJ & CO., Kingston, New York. *(solo exhibition)*
THE DEFINITIVE AMERICAN CONTEMPORARY QUILT, UNIVERSITY OF DELAWARE GALLERY, Newark, Delaware.

CONTEMPORARY TOTEMS, ELENA ZANG GALLERY, Woodstock, New York.
VISION QUEST, THE ART GALLERY, Cleveland State University, Cleveland, Ohio.

1991   *GROUP EXHIBITION,* WILLOUGHBY SHARP GALLERY, New York, New York.
THE DEFINITIVE AMERICAN CONTEMPORARY QUILT, FELICITA FOUNDATION FOR THE ARTS,
Escondido, California.
HUDSON VALLEY ARTISTS '91, "MYTH, SPIRITUALITY, and CULTURE," COLLEGE ART GALLERY, State
University of New York at New Paltz, New Paltz, New York.
SCARLET LETTERS, KLEINERT/ JAMES ARTS CENTER, Woodstock, New York.

1990   *THE DEFINITIVE AMERICAN CONTEMPORARY QUILT,* BERNICE STEINBAUM GALLERY, New York,
New York.
CHICAGO INTERNATIONAL ART EXPOSITION—NAVY PIER SHOW, DART GALLERY, Chicago, Illinois.

1989   *NEW ACQUISITIONS,* CINCINNATI ART MUSEUM, Cincinnati, Ohio.
CHICAGO INTERNATIONAL ART EXPOSITION—NAVY PIER SHOW, DART GALLERY, Chicago, Illinois.
JAN HARRISON, PASTEL PAINTINGS, THE STANLEY GALLERY, Norfolk, Virginia. *(solo exhibition)*

1988   *A PERILOUS EDEN,* CHIDLAW GALLERY, Art Academy of Cincinnati, Cincinnati, Ohio. *(solo exhibition)*
CHICAGO INTERNATIONAL ART EXPOSITION—NAVY PIER SHOW, DART GALLERY, Chicago, Illinois.
OBJECT.IMAGE.ICON, THE CONTEMPORARY ARTS CENTRE, Adelaide, Australia.

1987   *THE 1987 OHIO SELECTIONS—GRAPHICS,* THE DAYTON ART INSTITUTE, Dayton, Ohio.
DRAWINGS, TONI BIRCKHEAD GALLERY, Cincinnati, Ohio. *(four artists.)*
SELF-PORTRAITS, ART ACADEMY OF CINCINNATI, CARL SOLWAY GALLERY, Cincinnati, Ohio.

1986   *DIVINING HOUSE,* THE CONTEMPORARY ARTS CENTER, Cincinnati, Ohio. *Collaborative work with Alan
Baer, architect.*
NEW SITES/NEW WORK, The First San Jose Biennial, THE SAN JOSE INSTITUTE OF CONTEMPORARY
ART, San Jose, California.
INTERFACE: OUTSIDERS AND INSIDERS, OHIO UNIVERSITY, Lancaster, Ohio.

1985   *CONTEMPORARY WOMEN ARTISTS FROM THE PERMANENT COLLECTION,* MIAMI UNIVERSITY ART
MUSEUM, Oxford, Ohio.

1984   *NEW ACQUISITIONS,* THE OHIO STATE UNIVERSITY, Columbus, Ohio.

DRAWN TO CINCINNATI, THE CONTEMPORARY ARTS CENTER, Cincinnati, Ohio.

JAN HARRISON, GUND GALLERY, Ohio Arts Council, Columbus, Ohio. *(solo exhibition)*

FIGURATIVELY SPEAKING II, THE ART GALLERY, Cleveland State University, Cleveland, Ohio.

CINCINNATI SELECTIONS, 1984 CINCINNATI ART MUSEUM INVITATIONAL, Cincinnati, Ohio.

RECENT ACQUISITIONS, CINCINNATI ART MUSEUM, Cincinnati, Ohio.

1983   *JAN HARRISON, NEW WORK,* TONI BIRCKHEAD GALLERY, Cincinnati, Ohio. *(solo exhibition)*

THE BIG PICTURE, SEIGFRED GALLERY, OHIO UNIVERSITY, Athens, Ohio. *(four artists)*

JAN HARRISON, HOBART & WILLIAM SMITH COLLEGES, Geneva, New York. *(solo exhibition)*

THE 1983 OHIO SELECTION, THE DAYTON ART INSTITUTE, Dayton, Ohio.

1982   *OHIO SELECTIONS II,* NEW GALLERY OF CONTEMPORARY ART, Cleveland, Ohio.

FIGURE '82, THE CONTEMPORARY ARTS CENTER, Cincinnati, Ohio.

EMERGING TALENT (TEN OHIO ARTISTS), WRIGHT STATE UNIVERSITY, Dayton, Ohio. *(solo exhibition)*

1981   *SOLIDARITAT for SOLIDARNOSC,* Kassel, Germany.

CINCINNATI ART MUSEUM INVITATIONAL, CINCINNATI ART MUSEUM, Cincinnati, Ohio.

ANIMAL WISHES / ANIMAL DESIRES, C.A.G.E GALLERY, Cincinnati, Ohio. *(solo exhibition)*

1980   *CINCINNATI STORIES, An Exhibition of Narrative-Figurative Art,* SPACES, Cleveland, Ohio.

HELP, Exhibition of Mail Art and Multiples, Invitational, LOS ANGELES INSTITUTE OF CONTEMPORARY ART, Los Angeles, California.

FOUR ON FOURTH, TONI BIRCKHEAD GALLERY, Cincinnati, Ohio.

1979   *STRATEGIES,* THE CONTEMPORARY ARTS CENTER, Cincinnati, Ohio.

THE OTHER CHILD, WARSAW POLYTECHNIC, REMONT GALLERY, Warsaw, Poland.

CINCINNATI UNDEREXPOSED, TANGEMAN FINE ARTS GALLERY, University of Cincinnati, Ohio.

1978   *POSTERS, BOOKS, POSTCARDS—BY WOMEN,* THE WOMEN'S BUILDING, Los Angeles, California.

JAN HARRISON, PAINTINGS, MONTALVO CENTER FOR THE ARTS, Saratoga, California. *(solo exhibition)*

ARTWORDS AND BOOKWORKS, An International Exhibition of Recent Artists' Books and Ephemera, LOS ANGELES INSTITUTE OF CONTEMPORARY ART, Los Angeles, California.

1976   *THE PRINTED WORK/THE RECORDED WORK,* LA MAMELLE ARTS CENTER, San Francisco, California.

SELECTED BIBLIOGRAPHY:

Weintraub, Linda, "GENUS FUSION," ANIMAL.ANIMA.ANIMUS exhibition catalogue/book, Pori Art Museum Publications, Pori, Finland, FRAME Publications, Helsinki, Finland, 1998.

Majasaari, Marja-Liisa, "TEURASTUKSESTA LÖYTYY HUUMORIAKIN!," PÄIVYRI/KULTT, Finland, 6/16/98.

Linnala, Erkki, "LUOMAKUNNAN KRUUNU?" KULTTUURI, Satakunnan Kansa, Finland, 6/14/98.

Rice, Robin, "JAN HARRISON," THE BINNEWATER TIDES, Women's Studio Workshop, Rosendale, New York, Fall, 1998.

Tychostup, Lorna, "SPEAKING IN TONGUES," ANIMALIA ISSUE, CHRONOGRAM, New Paltz, New York, 3/98.

Raynor, Vivien, "WATER IS A SOURCE OF INSPIRATION FOR LANDSCAPE SCULPTURES," THE NEW YORK TIMES, New York, New York, 8/28/94.

Norklun, Kathi, "PERSONAL BEAST," WOODSTOCK TIMES, Woodstock, New York, 12/2/93.

Kolpan, Steven, "BEAST OF EDEN," WOODSTOCK TIMES, Woodstock, New York, 5/25/92.

Combs, Tram, "JAN HARRISON AT SUNNEN GALLERY," NOTICIAS DE ARTE, New York, New York, 5/92.

Lauter, Estella, "WOMEN AS MYTHMAKERS REVISITED," QUADRANT, THE JOURNAL OF CONTEMPORARY JUNGIAN THOUGHT, Volume 23, Number 1, New York, New York.

Pollak, Ann, "MYTHS FOR OUR TIME," DIALOGUE, Columbus, Ohio, 5/89.

Schwindler, Gary J., "A PERILOUS EDEN: Pastel Drawings by Jan Harrison," DIALOGUE, Columbus, Ohio, 9/88.

Schwindler, Gary J., "JAN HARRISON," NEW ART EXAMINER, Chicago, Illinois, 9/88.

Findsen, Owen, "ARTIST HARRISON'S FACES, FIGURES...," THE CINCINNATI ENQUIRER, Cincinnati, Ohio, 6/88.

Riley, Jan, "DRAWING," Toni Birckhead Gallery, Cincinnati, 27 June - 30 July, DIALOGUE, Columbus, Ohio, 1/88.

Small, Janus, "JAN HARRISON—Paintings and Drawings," DIALOGUE, Columbus, Ohio, 3/84.

Riley, Jan, "JAN HARRISON, Toni Birckhead Gallery," NEW ART EXAMINER, Chicago, Illinois, 12/83.

Franz, Gina, "FIGURATIVELY SPEAKING," NEW ART EXAMINER, Chicago, Illinois, 4/83.

Fryer Kohles, Jeanne, "CINCY ELEVEN," DIALOGUE, Columbus, Ohio, 5/82.

Foreman, B.J., "FIGURAL ART STAR OF A SHOW," THE CINCINNATI POST, Cincinnati, Ohio, 5/82.

Hoxie, Elizabeth, "AUDREY SKUODAS/ JAN HARRISON—TEN SOLO EXHIBITIONS (PART I,)" NEW ART EXAMINER, Chicago, Illinois, 4/82.

Bloomfield, Maureen, "ENDING THE SILENCE," DIALOGUE, Columbus, Ohio, 4/82.

Collings, Betty, "JAN HARRISON," Ten Solo Exhibitions—Emerging Talent, DIALOGUE, Columbus, Ohio, 2/82.

Moore, John, "CINCINNATI STORIES," DIALOGUE, Columbus, Ohio, 10/80.

Munro, Eleanor, "THE VIRTUES OF STAYING AT HOME," CINCINNATI MAGAZINE, Cincinnati, Ohio, 8/80.

Day, Holliday T., "MIDWEST ART: A SPECIAL REPORT," ART IN AMERICA, New York, New York, 7/79.

Lippard, Lucy, Article in CHRYSALIS, Los Angeles, California, 1978.

SELECTED PUBLIC COLLECTIONS:

Arco Center for the Visual Arts, *Los Angeles, California.*
Cincinnati Art Museum, *Cincinnati, Ohio.*
Cincinnati Bell Corporation, *Cincinnati, Ohio.*
The Dayton Art Institute, *Dayton, Ohio.*
Samuel Dorsky Museum of Art, *New Paltz, New York.*
Scripps Howard Corporation, *Cincinnati, Ohio.*
University of Cincinnati, College of DAAP, *Cincinnati, Ohio.*
The Wexner Center for the Arts, *Columbus, Ohio.*
Women's Studio Workshop, *Rosendale, New York.*

SELECTED PRIVATE COLLECTIONS:

Alan D. Baer, Kingston, New York.
Toni Birckhead, Cincinnati, Ohio.
Susan Dickson, Chicago, Illinois.
Susan DiPasquale, Columbus, Ohio.
B.J. & Arthur Foreman, Cincinnati, Ohio.
John Henderson & Richard DuBeshter, Chicago, Illinois.
Peter Huttinger & Vicki Mansoor, Cincinnati, Ohio.
Catherine Keller & Jason Starr, New York, New York.
Dr. Wayne P. Lawson, Columbus, Ohio.
Sergiu Luca & Margaret LeCompte, Boulder, Colorado.
Ann Meranus, Cincinnati, Ohio.
Nancy Moore, New York, New York.
Derek & Linda Pardee, Colts Neck, New Jersey.
Dr. & Mrs. Victor Pollak, Boulder, Colorado.
Dr. Susan Righi, Kingston, New York.
Dr. Naomi Schechter, New York, New York.
Carolee Schneemann, New Paltz, New York.
Ellen Sribnick & Pat Clarke, Rosendale, New York.
Bernice Steinbaum, Miami, Florida.
Dr. Jeffrey Scott Viglielmo & Dr. Maureen Wright, Kingston, New York.
Tony Walsh & Maureen France, Cincinnati, Ohio.
James Yarosh, Highland, New Jersey.

SELECTED FELLOWSHIPS:

Ohio Arts Council Individual Artist Fellowship
for years 1988, 1985, 1983
Ohio Arts Council New Works Grant,
(for collaboration with Alan Baer, architect) for year 1986

EDUCATION:

M.A., *1976,* San Jose State University, *San Jose, California*
B.F.A., *1967,* University of Georgia, *Athens, Georgia*

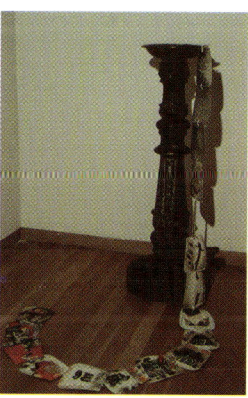

Tongue Drawing
1979
Installation: 40 x 24 inches
size of drawing: 94 x 4½ inches
mixed media on waterproofed bristolboard,
attached to drinking water fountain.
The Contemporary Arts Center, Cincinnati, Ohio
Collection: Alan D. Baer, Kingston, New York

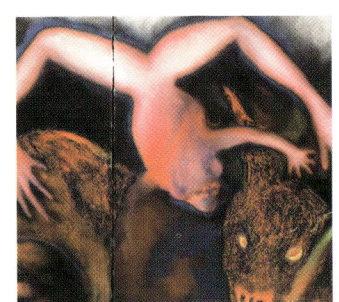

My other tongue sits in the very back

and flips over.